MW00669092

PIZZA AT THE PASSION PIT.

It's still early in the evening, but circa 1950s automobiles are beginning to gather at the Miracle Mile Drive In — a number of them occupied by young couples as enamored with each other as the double feature. Carolyn Hoge (on the left) and her fellow unknown concessionaire will be serving pizza to some of them. Carolyn worked here during her summer break in 1956, baking pizzas at the concession stand for her Aunt Phyllis Ann and Uncle Dominici D'Lelles. *Submitted by Carolyn (Hoge) Pietrzak.*

IN SERVICE TO THOSE IN NEED

The Daughters of Rebekah was the female auxiliary of the International Order of Odd Fellows, founded in the U.S. in the late 1800s. Lodge No. 197 in Lucas County, like its counterparts around the country, was dedicated to performing charitable works for those in need. Ed Hulce and Molly (Hulce) Pocock provide this 1920s photo of the group which includes their grandmother, Nellie "Babe" Hulce, sitting fourth from the right in the front row.

TOLEDO

Our Life, Our Times, Our Town, Vol. III

1800s – 1970 Toledo, Ohio

John Robinson Block
Publisher & Editor in Chief, The Blade

Joseph H. Zerbey, IV
Vice President & General Manager

Kelly J. Norwood
Project Manager

Sara E. Welborn
Creative Director/Graphic Designer

THE BLADE
toledoblade.com®

COVER PHOTOGRAPH.
Toledo Marine Terminal, 1955.
Photo courtesy of The Toledo Lucas County Public Library.

TOLEDO'S FINEST EXPORT.

A Willys Jeep CJ-5 was suspended from a cargo crane at the Toledo Marine Terminal across from downtown Toledo in 1955, its first year of production. Thanks to Hickman Price, Jr., president of Willys-Overland Export Company, it might have been headed to Bangkok to help deliver Coca-Cola, to Chile for herding cattle, or to India for a resettlement project.

After WWII, Willys-Overland shifted some of its production to civilian/passenger cars, where the competition was fierce. But Willys-Overland's most avid fans – the soldiers, farmers and government officials who had seen what the Jeep could do in the worst conditions – were buying military Jeeps for everything from farm work to replacing railroad engines (in Burma) and fire pumpers (like the Jeep "Bombero" in Guatemala).

The "workhorse" Jeep was even credited with replacing the ox, mule and caribou in agricultural work in many third-world countries. So when Price became president of Willys-Overland Export Co. in 1952, he began a series of "Jeep caravans," demonstrations of the vehicle's amazing, real-world capabilities in Latin America, Central and South America, and the Far East. By 1957, Willys-Overland had dealer/distributors in 40 countries, from Austria to the Belgian Congo, and from Norway to Saudi Arabia. They shipped from the Toledo Marine Terminal, now the site of The Docks row of restaurants.

Copyright © 2007 by The Blade
ISBN 978-0-9770681-2-8
Published by The Blade
A Block Communications Company
541 North Superior Street
Toledo OH 43660
Printed in the United States of America

For General Information, Customer Service, and Orders Contact:
Telephone   419.724.6545
                800.245.3317
FAX   419.724.6526
E-Mail   historybook@toledoblade.com

FOREWORD

Thank you, Toledo! Again, we asked you to pour through your albums and shoeboxes for photographic mementoes you would be willing to share – and you came through in unprecedented fashion. Frankly, our first two editions of "Toledo, Our Life, Our Times, Our Town" were filled with so many unique views of our community, we thought nothing more could surprise us. We were wrong.

Today, I proudly introduce the final, most revealing volume in our popular series, spotlighting eight decades in our city's evolution, from the burgeoning 1890s through the turbulent 1960s. One look and you will find this book's heart beats as strongly as its predecessors. Each page reverberates with images of a way of life we thought we would never see again: Our great, great grandparents eking out a pioneer's existence in a rough and tumble town. Our great grandparents marching off to war to defend the lifestyle their parents had built. Our grandparents founding fledgling businesses to support a growing economy. Our parents – or perhaps ourselves – young idealistic boomers with the dream of creating a fair, more tolerant world.

Over three hundred Toledo-area residents contributed to this photographic history, sharing nearly six hundred treasured snapshots. Each submission was evaluated for its importance to its time period; each photo left behind was done so with regret – for all were small mirrors reflecting who we had been and what we had become. We hope you enjoy our final selections, and that Volume III of "Toledo, Our Life, Our Times, Our Town" becomes a valued keepsake.

Share Volumes I, II and III with your family. The times captured within these covers are gone. Only the memories remain. Travel through them with pride, as we did. It's a journey of a lifetime – and one we can never take again.

Joseph H. Zerbey, IV
Vice President & General Manager
The Blade

ACKNOWLEDGEMENT

History is the story of our lives. This book of photographs, and the two that came before, weave a tapestry of time that tells the story of Toledo and its people in a way that would never otherwise have occurred.

We thank our readers again for sharing with us their photos, their stories, their lives, so that we might ultimately share them with you. In some cases, time or misfortune have damaged the photos that appear herein. We are grateful that they survived and consider them all the more precious for it.

Much of the information with each photo was provided by its owner. Dates, places and background information for some photos verified and/or clarified through research in The Blade library. But while newspapers document our lives one day or one week at a time, newspapers alone cannot tell the full story of a family or a community. For that reason, we give special acknowledgement to the Local History and Genealogy Department at the Main branch of the Toledo-Lucas County Public Library for their dedication to preserving local history, their depth of knowledge, their invaluable assistance, and their generosity.

We hope that these volumes have helped you reconnect with memories, with families, with neighbors and neighborhoods, and with the stories of how they built the towns we call home. This is your story.

Writing and Research
Denise Meyer
Larry R. Michaels
Doreen Robideaux

Contributing Writers
Kelly J. Norwood	**Rolf Scheidel**
Jane Bryan Welborn	**Janene Fentress**
Sara E. Welborn	

Contributing Graphic Designer
Phillip D. Long

Coordinator
Matthew T. Lentz

Additional Thanks
Michael Lora, *Manager of The Toledo-Lucas County Public Library, Local History and Genealogy Department,*
Donna Christian, Ann Hurley, Irene Martin, Gregory Miller and Laura Voelz

The Blade Library, Toledo Lucas County Port Authority,
Tedd Long, The Toledo Firefighter's Museum

John R. Husman, Ron Szemanski, *The great, knowledgeable Blade retirees*

100 YEARS AND COUNTING.

When Fred Titgemeier opened this feed and flour store in 1888, he had no way of knowing it would become a South Toledo landmark. Located on the southwest corner of Western Avenue and Marion Street, the business had been in the same location and in the same family for four generations. Here, patrons gather outside the store to purchase hay, straw, oats, flour and livestock feed. Notice the delivery wagon in the side yard. It was pulled by Tom and Jerry, two horses that in their time became as well-known as the store itself, inspiring countless offers to buy them, including interest from the Toledo Fire Department and mortician H.H. Birkenkamp. *Submitted by the Titgemeier family.*

ICE AND COAL: DELIVERY THE GOAL.

The Elevator Ice & Coal Company, with offices at 539 Ontario at Beech Street, delivered ice and coal from its warehouses along the riverfront. Here, in 1892, driver William G. Basilius stands at the front of his delivery wagon where Cherry, Summit and St. Clair streets then merged. A helper is perched at the back, ready to roll. The monument behind them honors Toledoan Major General James Blair Steedman, U.S. Army Commander during the Civil War. The statue was dedicated in 1887, just four years after Steedman died and a few years before this photo was taken. *Submitted by Henry's grandson, Gerald Moore.*

FIRST CLASS.

John Meister was born in Switzerland and immigrated to Toledo in 1867. Three years later he opened a butcher shop and meat market at Segur and Broadway. He is seen here riding high in his market delivery wagon in front of his Spencer Street home, circa 1890. John had good reason to be proud. His establishment would be praised in Bend of the River as a "first class butcher and meat shop" with a "superior assortment of fresh, salt and smoked meats." *Submitted by John's great, great grandchildren, John and Dreama Schiffer.*

A PLEASANT AFTERNOON

Mary Maher (Keiseger) and her baby relax on the porch of their home in what is now known as the St. Patrick's historic area of Toledo. A man identified simply as "uncle" waits in the horse-drawn buggy. *Submitted by Mary's granddaughter, Sue Dial.*

BELLY UP TO THE BAR, BOYS.

At age 16, Tom Boatfield immigrated to the U.S., where he met and married Dolly Ripus. Together they had four children, Wally, Verna, Norma and Bob. Supporting them wasn't easy, so Tom tackled a number of money-making ventures, including barkeep. By 1895, his saloon was a thriving business on Bancroft and Lagrange Streets. He stands in front of its open door, dressed in the traditional white bar apron, his patrons waiting to enter for a cool brew. *Submitted by Tom's great grandson, Dennis Johnson.*

LEWIS' LIBATIONS.

Pub owner Nathan James Lewis sizes up the patrons enjoying a libation in his 1892 establishment, once located at Central near Albion. Note the selection of savories posted on the wall. A hearty ham sandwich would have set you back a nickel, while beans cost an extravagant 10¢. *Submitted by Robert Livingston, grandson of Nathan Lewis.*

3

WORLD FAMOUS.

The Toledo State Hospital earned worldwide acclaim for its innovations. It opened in 1889, when most "homes for the insane" resembled prisons. Toledo's approach proved the value of the "cottage system," in which patients had more freedom, gentle care and healthy activity that included team sports. Ed Breniff (front, left of sign) played on this Toledo State Hospital baseball team in 1897, winning 31 out of 36 games. The hospital sat on 600 acres, which included the cottages, a hospital, baseball diamond, 900-seat auditorium and four man-made lakes, a golf course and wooded grounds that were created by the patients themselves. They also worked a 500+ acre farm raising cows, pigs, chickens and crops and had their own dairy. *Submitted by Ed's grandson, Dennis DeViney.*

WELCOME TO THE BEER GARDEN.

At 2102 Walnut St., where Moore Street intersected, Bernhard "Barney" and Magdelena "Lena" (Wernert) Thomas ran a grocery store with a beer garden patio. Attached to the patio is a shelter for the carriage (right). Posing for this 1895 photo are, from left, Mark Knowles, a neighbor at 2515 Walnut St.; George Clement Wernert, nephew of Barney and Lena; Lena and Barney Thomas, and Nick Spinner, a neighbor at 2114 Walnut St. The store and saloon remained in operation until 1912. *Submitted by the Thomases' granddaughter, Judy Shook.*

A GIFT OF MEMORIES.

Teacher R.H. Stoldt gave his students a special gift for Christmas in 1899: a formal portrait of the entire class taken at Sherman School. The young man seated second from left next to Stoldtz is Walter Hartung, Sr. In later years, he would further his education at the Toledo Medical College, and become Toledo's Health Commissioner from 1943-1957. *Submitted by Walter's granddaughters, Mary Ann Kurtz and Martha Frost.*

WORKING FROM HOME ON FASSETT.

Working out of your house isn't a modern concept. Henry Bauer's barber shop was in his home at 208 Fassett Street. Note the wooden barber poles, one at the street and the other hanging on the door frame. His family poses outside the residence, from left to right: daughter Dora, son Albert, Henry, youngest daughter Mary, and wife Katherine. The wooden sidewalks shown in this circa 1897 photo are gone, but the Bauer's old home still stands today. *Submitted by Henry's great granddaughter, Mary Lou Stripling.*

POSH ACCOMODATIONS.

This photo of the Hotel LaLond has seen better days. The hotel itself never saw better than those in which it flourished. Proprietor Thomas LaLonde immigrated to the U.S. from Montreal, Canada at age 20. He launched his first lodging endeavor, the Hotel Montreal, on Ottawa Street near the Oliver House in 1886, followed in later years by the Clifton House on St. Clair Street between Jefferson Avenue and Monroe Street, and then the LaLond on the corner of St. Clair and LaFayette in the early 1900s. Eventually the building would be sold to the St. Clair Machine Company, and finally demolished in the late 1960s to make way for a new highway system. Thomas LaLond died November 7, 1910 at the age of 66. The family's history in the Toledo hotel industry would be preserved by his granddaughter, the late Mary Lynch, an employee of The Toledo Blade Circulation Department during the 1960s. *Submitted by Edward J. Kelb, Sr., great grandson of Thomas LaLonde.*

MEN IN HATS.

The set could have been decorated for The Sting: a pressed-tin ceiling, bucolic mural wall mural, spittoons for each customer, and men ONLY at the bar, dressed in their best attire. The only things missing are Robert Redford and Paul Newman. In reality, it is Casey's Saloon, located on Erie Street between Jefferson and Monroe circa 1900. *Submitted by Ed Grohowski.*

OVER-ACHIEVING UNDERTAKER.

Hoeflinger & Co Undertaking opened the first funeral business in East Toledo on or near Main Street in 1877. Twenty-three years later, they built a larger space at 201 Platt Street. Their elegant funeral wagon is shown here in front of the new building. Theodore Hoeflinger (in the button-studded suit) is believed to be riding on top. The sign on the side of the building reads, "Undertaking, Livery Tack, Boarding & Feeding, Sales Stable." The business has been in business for over 130 years, and operates today as Hoeflinger-Bolander Funeral Home, 3500 Navarre Avenue, Oregon. *Submitted by Jim Bolander*

FIRE AND ICE.

On January 31, 1901, an early morning fire destroyed a building occupied by The Dolphin White Lead and Color Works at 28 Summit Street. The fire department's efforts were severely hampered by the intense cold and inaccessibility of fire hydrants buried under ashes and debris. In this view of the back of the damaged buildings, tugs and steamers are seen tied up along the dock on Swan Creek. One of the tugs, the "E.G. Ashley," was owned by Edward G. Ashley who operated a grocery and meat market in an adjoining building. *Photo submitted and caption written by Rolf Scheidel.*

SOUTH ST. CLAIR SURFACING.
The original building of the American Floor Surfacing Machine
Company is shown in this early photograph taken about 1903. The
company was incorporated in February 1903, and was located at
518 South St. Clair Street. They manufactured industrial floor maintenance machines and portable tools. *Submitted by Marcella DeMars,
who worked there for 53 years.*

RELIGIOUSLY PRESERVED.
The interior of St. Francis de Sales church at Cherry and
Superior Streets is captured in all its grandeur in this photo
from a 1903 First Communion memento. The card features
a portrait of Paul Maher as a young man, and a photo of the
church's pastor, Reverend John T. O'Connell. *Submitted by
Paul's daughter, Sue Dial.*

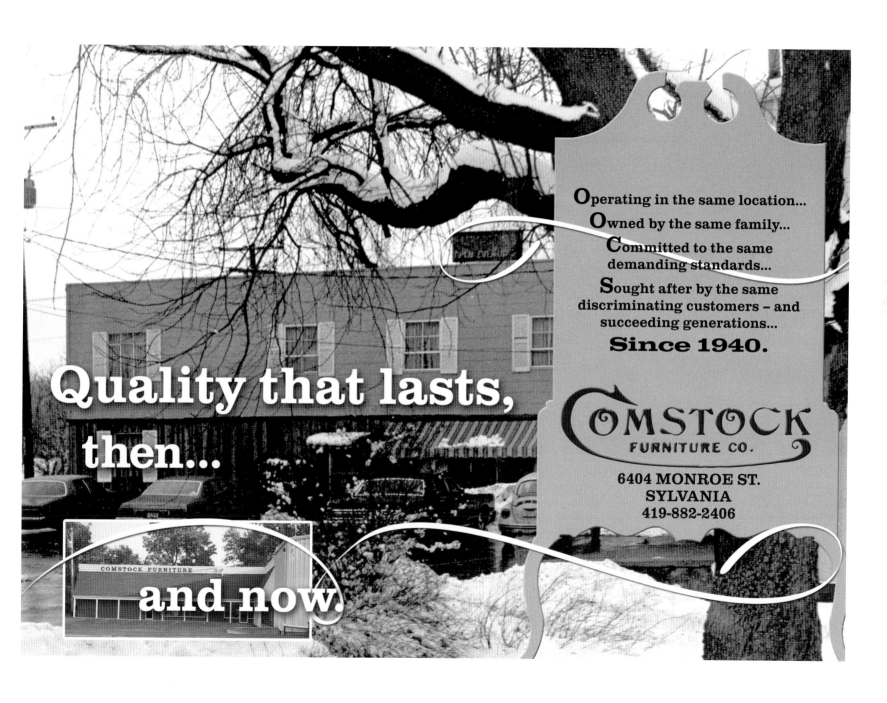

Quality that lasts, then...

and now.

Operating in the same location...

Owned by the same family...

Committed to the same demanding standards...

Sought after by the same discriminating customers – and succeeding generations...

Since 1940.

COMSTOCK FURNITURE CO.

6404 MONROE ST.
SYLVANIA
419-882-2406

COMSTOCK FURNITURE

AH, SERENITY!

Believed by some to be Toledo's first official recreational area, City Park was established in 1871 on Nebraska Avenue at City Park in the Lenk's Hill area. Numerous Irish and German immigrants who settled in Lenk's Hill came here to relax alongside the lagoon. After a hard week of working on the canals and railroads, it was a much-needed respite. This circa 1905 photo was probably taken to commemorate the lagoon's recent construction. *Submitted by Virginia Keaton, from the estates of Charles and Paul Morgan.*

ROSS/FORD SCHOOL.

The town of Rossford was the creation of Edward Ford. He bought a piece of land large enough to build his glass plant and a small town around it. Named for his wife (whose maiden name was Ross) and himself, in 1898 Ford laid out the tracts and built homes for plant employees (which sold for up to $1,500). The plant provided electricity and water to the homes. He founded the Rossford Savings Bank, one of two banks in Rossford, and he built the Edward Ford Club (a community center) and the Rossford Public School, seen here in 1903 with about 100 students. By 1921 it was the third largest school in the county. *Submitted by Glenna Ford.*

ALL HANDS TOGETHER.

Pitching in to position the cornerstone, Grand Master W.A. Belt helps from the stage as others lend a hand from below. The Free and Accepted Masons were the largest of the many "secret societies" that were as common at the turn of the century as parent-teacher organizations (PTOs) and neighborhood associations are today. Their members have included Benjamin Franklin, the Rev. Jesse Jackson, Russian poet Alexander Pushkin, U.S. Supreme Court Justice Thurgood Marshall, Sir Arthur Conan Doyle (Sherlock Holmes's creator) and Wolfgang Amadeus Mozart. In this photo, the building in the background is the local home of the Grand Army of the Republic, a fraternal group started by veterans of the Civil War. *Submitted by Byron L. Stickles.*

WORLD CLASS SWEETS ON ADAMS STREET.

Hoffman's Fine Confectionery and Ice Cream Parlor was more than a sweet shop; it was a destination. John Hoffman's first shop was at 423 Adams St. He enlarged it and redecorated, adding an entrance on Superior Street. The candy was made on the second floor, which also had a bakery. Hoffman had pursued a career as a fine watchmaker in his native Switzerland, but failing eyesight soon made him turn to the family business – candies. Customers ordered Hoffman's candies from as far away as Austria and France. *Submitted by Marty Uhl, grandson of Clement Uhl, founder of The Toledo Metal Furniture Company which designed and built the counter stools.*

THE FAMILY LEE.

Joseph Lee is at the center of this family in more ways than one. He's the patriarch of this hard-working clan, all of whom established homes in Toledo's South End. Both he and his namesake, Joseph M., worked for the Wabash Railroad, the father as an engineer; the son as a checker. Pictured here in 1904 are Lee family members (standing, from left) George (behind his wife and child), Joseph M. (behind his wife and child), Jim, mother Vivian (Westendorf) Lee, Fred, Frank and Charles. Seated, from center, father Joseph, Sr., with baby John, Nell and Robert. *Submitted by Vivian Westendorf.*

A CORNERSTONE OF FAITH.

Hundreds of soon-to-be parishioners gather to watch the cornerstone laying at St. Charles Borromeo Catholic Church on July 19, 1903. Bishop Horstmann assists with a blessing. The 16th church of the Catholic faith in Toledo, St. Charles Borromeo was completed in October 1904 and dedicated October 16 of the same year. *Submitted by Virginia Keaton from the estates of Charles and Paul Morgan.*

TOLEDO'S TOBACCO PLANT.

These ladies are employees of the J.F. Zahn Tobacco Company in 1905. Agnes Kujawa (later Demski) and sister Mary (later Czerniak) pose in the top row, third and fourth from left, respectively. They processed loose-leaf chewing tobacco at the factory on Council Street off Detroit Avenue. Four years later, Swayne Field ballpark will be built right next door, putting the plant just beyond the left-field fence. In 1911, the company will be purchased by The Pinkerton Tobacco Company, makers of the well-known Red Man brand of "smokeless" tobacco. *Submitted by Mary's daughter, Rita (Czerniak) Marczak.*

PRODUCE APLENTY.

There's plenty of fresh produce at the C. B. Downing Cash Grocery, 302 Indiana Avenue. Business is good in 1906 when Charles Bruff and his wife, Anna, (both former Clay Township teachers) stand outside the store for this photo. They're keeping an eye on little June, age 3, in hat and cloak nearby. *Submitted by June's son, C. Thomas Siglar, and his wife, Alice.*

13

TOLEDO'S GARMENT DISTRICT.

Morris Cohn (left) stands at the entrance to his menswear and tailoring shop at 617 Cherry St. in 1905. His son, Carl (right), was a student when this was taken. Louis Cohn clerked at the store and boarded with Morris. In 1893 the shop was listed under Friedericka Cohn, his wife, and Morris was listed as manager. By 1904 the shop was under Morris's name. The Cohns' shop was one of many clothiers on Cherry Street at the time. There were six others from 328 to 905 Cherry St. and three more in the four blocks beyond. *Submitted by Fred Cohn, Morris's grandson and Carl's nephew.*

A MAN WITH A PLAN.

Charles Bruff Downing stands beside his delivery wagon in 1905. He has a grocery business at 302 Indiana Ave. with a home upstairs where he and his wife, Anna (nee Avery), are raising a family. He also has bigger plans for his future. In 1913 he will be one of the graduates of Toledo Medical School. *Submitted by grandson C. Thomas Siglar and wife Alice.*

POISED TO LEARN.

Learning was serious business in 1907, as suggested in this photo of the sixth-grade class at Sts. Peter and Paul Catholic Church on St. Clair Street. Long before jeans, T-shirts, sandals and streaked hair became the mainstream, neatly coifed students headed off to school in long skirts and blouses, button-down shirts, ties and polished shoes. Like her fellow classmates, Eleanor Geck (row nearest the window, second seat) is poised to learn. *Submitted by Ruth Sturtz, daughter of Eleanor Geck.*

BEFORE WESTGATE.

Joe and Ursula Meiring and their daughter and son-in-law, Lena and August Schetter, purchased 120 acres of land at the corner of Secor Road and Central Avenue in 1875. In 1905, Ursula, then a widow, divided her 100 acres among her children. In this 1908 photo, Lena makes apple butter with her daughter, Minnie, in what is still a bucolic setting. Before long, however, the family would sell the property to Welles Bowen for development. Roads were graded but not yet paved when the Great Depression brought the project to a halt. Decades later in the mid-1950s it would become Westgate Village Shopping Center. The new Costco store now stands on the site of the Schetter home shown here. *Submitted by Marge Ainsworth, daughter of Minnie (Schetter) Linenkugel.*

CHARLES A. COTTRILL, COMMUNITY LEADER.

Charles A. Cottrill, a nationally known politician and leader of the black community in Toledo in the early years of the 20th century, posed for this picture in his real estate office in the Nicholas Building, now Fifth Third Center. Cottrill attended Toledo's old Central High School on Michigan Street at a time when few people attended high school. He graduated at the age of 17 as the president of the class of 1881. Thereafter, he was employed in the offices of the Ohio Secretary of State, the Lucas County Treasurer and the Lucas County Recorder. He served as the president of the Toledo branch of the N.A.A.C.P. and as an officer of many fraternal organizations. Following 18 years in the Lucas County Recorder's office, Cottrill accepted an appointment from President William Howard Taft as the Collector of Revenue in Honolulu, Hawaii (1911-15). Pictures of President Taft and Cottrill and his family in Honolulu can be seen hanging on the wall of his real estate office. When he died in 1924, at age 60, Cottrill was the only black 33rd degree Mason in Toledo. *Submitted and caption written by Rolf Scheidel.*

FEMALE PIONEERS.

There were only three female students in this graduating class of the Toledo Medical College. Women doctors were still a rare breed in 1908. The group is seated for a class portrait in the amphitheater inside the college at Cherry and Page streets. But don't let their stoic expressions fool you. They had quite a sense of humor – note the skeleton in the front row, right. Future state health commissioner Walter Hartung, Sr., seated in the second row from the bottom behind the skeleton, is also pictured. *Submitted by Walter's granddaughters, Mary Ann Kurtz and Martha Frost.*

GENERATIONS OF LEARNING.

Back in 1893, Detroit Avenue School was a new facility with 36 rooms – large for a new school in this area at that time. Jay Brower, fourth row, second from left, stands with his classmates for this 1908 graduating class photo. By 1915, the community had outgrown the original building and a new school was built on the same site, named for U.S. President Abraham Lincoln. It has distinguished itself in many ways through the years and still does today as the Lincoln Academy for Boys. *Submitted by Jay's great-niece, Jeanne Weckerlin.*

EARLY OREGON SCHOOL.

This Gardner School building was already ten years old when this photo was taken in 1909. The original one-room school had been built facing Coy Road at a cost of $325. It was razed in 1898 and the new brick school was built (for under $1,000) on the same site, but facing Pickle Road. Miss Douglas (back, far left) taught all grades. Laura Schardt (later Cousino), second row, second from left, was a third or fourth grader at this time. In 1918, Gardner students were moved to the larger Brandville School. Too small for teaching larger multiple grades, Gardner School was closed in 1924. *Submitted by Laura's son, Larry Cousino.*

FRESH TO YOUR DOOR.

William Gable, the gentleman in the apron, was one of several Tiedtke's delivery men in 1910. The convenience of deliveries was a godsend, especially for mothers with several children, for whom a trip downtown took time away from children and chores. Although it was a headache for the Tiedtke brothers for several reasons, they knew the value of doing whatever it took for their customers. They even delivered by boat to cargo ships as they sailed by on the Maumee. The Adams Express Company in the background is one of several messenger firms that provided delivery service for businesses. *Submitted by William's granddaughter, Marjorie Scalia.*

"BEST DRUGS. BEST PRICES."

If the sign on the wall didn't make it clear, the name on the door would. Hanf was a well-known name in pharmacy in Toledo for over three-quarters of a century. German immigrant Louis Michael Hanf and his family operated pharmacies in the area for 78 years and at one time boasted six locations. This store at Monroe Street and Lawrence Avenue was originally Russell Drugs, before the Hanfs purchased it and changed it to L.M. Hanf in 1910. *Submitted by Rhonda (Hanf) Hayes and family.*

PUMPED ABOUT HIS JOB.

Mitchel Aubry worked as a volunteer firefighter for six months before being hired by the Toledo Fire Department on August 15, 1909. Assigned badge number 62, he worked at various stations over the course of his career, rising to lieutenant on December 25, 1918, and becoming a captain before his death in 1936. He is seen in this circa 1910 photo driving the horse-drawn steamer engine. The steam pumper was coal fired and, when at its hottest, was pumped by hand to create pressure that would draw water through the hose. The department's first motorized pumper engine was not purchased until 1915. *Submitted by Mitchel's grandson, Jim Aubry Garbe.*

KNEE HIGH.

Toledo Beach was the place to cool down on a hot summer's day in 1911. Helen Sommers (far right), her sister, Myrtle (third from right), and their friends show off their stylish bathing attire for the camera. Got to love those bathing caps! *Submitted by Sue Dial.*

19

DAPPER JOHN'S DRY GOODS.

John Doan could be a living, breathing advertisement for the quality of goods found inside his store. Doan's Dry Goods located on Phillips Avenue circa 1910 specialized in stationary, pharmaceuticals, toys and, as his attire proves, the finest in men's furnishings. That is his daughter, Nonnie Doan, smiling at his side. *Submitted by John's granddaughter, Norene Collins McCollam.*

THE BODY OF KNOWLEDGE.

These students are attending a freshman anatomy class in 1910 at the Toledo Medical College located at Page and Cherry streets. Yes, they are standing around a cadaver on the table. This photo appears in *The History of the Toledo Medical College,* by Max T. Schnitker, MD and Walter H. Hartung, Jr, MD. The students are, from left, Nicholas Seybold, John French, Cleal Hissong, Ray Bowen, Theodore Griest, unidentified, Otto Muhme, Hoyt Meader, Frank G. Kreft, Roscoe "Clell" Huffman, Verne Mellott and John Walter Baldwin. Due to financial reasons, they were the last class to graduate from the Toledo Medical College before it was absorbed into Toledo University. *Submitted by Alice and C. Thomas Siglar.*

THE START OF A SUCCESSFUL CAREER.

These medical residents stand on the steps of the old St. Vincent Hospital on Cherry Street, circa 1912. From left to right they are Walter Hartung, Sr., Barry Hein and Thomas Higgins. (The fourth doctor is unknown.) Walter Hartung would enjoy a highly successful career in medicine: He held the post of Lucas County Coroner from 1916 to 1920, was appointed state health commissioner by Governor Martin Davey in 1934, and served as the City of Toledo's health commissioner from 1943-1957. Today's sprawling state-of-the-art St. Vincent Mercy Medical Center sits on the same site as the original hospital shown here. *Submitted by Walter's granddaughters, Mary Ann Kurtz and Martha Frost.*

A TRIM AND A TUNE.

Julian Romanowski, in front of his business with his young son, operated a side-by-side barbershop and jewelry store at 321 Warsaw St. in old North Toledo. The business encompassed the sale of guns, phonographs and musical instruments. And in his Polish community, that definitely included accordions (there are three in the window). By 1922 he was strictly a jeweler. But in 1930 – after the stock market crashed – he went back to barbering, work that was more likely to enable him to feed his children. *Submitted by Julian's granddaughter, Dyane Skunda.*

FOLLOW THE NEBRASKA BRICK ROAD.

Brick roads, like the one seen in this circa 1912 photo of Nebraska Avenue (at Division Street), were commonplace in Toledo and in cities all across the U.S. Unlike their predecessor, the single-lane dirt trail, brick roads were much better suited to meeting the demands placed on them by expanding urban centers and, in particular, the rapidly increasing number of automobiles in the first part of the 20th century. It wouldn't be until the 1950s that bigger and heavier vehicles, greater traffic and rising street-repair costs would be responsible for quaint paved roadways largely having been replaced by concrete and asphalt. *Submitted by Ruth Sturtz.*

PRODUCTION PRIDE.

A 1912 vehicle has rolled off the line at Toledo's Willys-Overland plant, and the crew responsible for its finished production halts long enough to pose for this photo. Fred J. Trost is a member of this final assembly team in Department 10. He is the mustached man in the hat standing midway back on the right. *Submitted by Carlene Trost, granddaughter by marriage to Fred Trost.*

A BOY WITH A VISION.

Twelve-year-old William Perry Burroughs, shown here in 1913, may be a mere youngster on the outside, but inside lies a man with a mission; a man whose drive and dedication will forever change politics and the black man's role in governing Lucas County. After completing 11th grade at Waite High School, Burroughs became active in Democratic party affairs. As the first black elected Eighth Ward Committeeman, he stirred political activism in other blacks, who went on to vie for similar positions. He was elected delegate to the 1944 and 1948 Democratic national conventions and, in 1949, helped organize the Federated County Democrats in Ohio. But Burroughs also championed causes at home, contributing to charities and helping provide food and clothing to needy families. To this day, the William Perry Burroughs Democratic Women's Club uses his name in honor of his service and accomplishments. *Submitted by Grace Edwards.*

FEARING FILL.
Captured on film after approximately two months of digging, the railroad overpass on Fearing Boulevard between Wayne Street (now Airport Highway) and Hill Avenue is taking shape. The excess soil from the construction was loaded onto railcars and transported down the line to Shasta Street, where it was used to fill in a ravine. *Submitted by Virginia Keaton, from the estates of Charles and Paul Morgan.*

JUST ADD WATER.
The Wilkinsons proudly display the boat they had just finished building in this 1913 photograph taken in front of Clarence Wilkinson's home at 1870 Erie St. Pictured left to right are Benoni James Wilkinson, the father; Clarence Wilkinson, Albert Wilkinson, Walter Wilkinson, and an unknown man. It is also unknown who Lola was. *Submitted by Kathleen Stein.*

MYRTLE on BEACH.

Bathing beauty Myrtle Sommers lounges in the surf at Toledo Beach in this 1915 photo. Obviously, with swim dresses like this one, sunscreen would have been an option rather than a necessity in the early 20th century. *Submitted by Sue Dial.*

TIME MARCHES ON.

A parade makes its way down Madison Avenue in downtown Toledo in this circa 1915 photo. The Spitzer and Gardner buildings are visible just behind the marchers and horseback riders. The large blur to the right in this photo is the head of a female office worker who is leaning out a third-floor window. She is just one of many who have deserted their desks to enjoy the festivities. *Submitted by Jan Ehrmann.*

THE ART OF RELAXATION.

The Old Newsboys take time away from their charitable works to perform on the steps of the Toledo Museum of Art on June 20, 1915. The band was a popular attraction in the early 20th century, but the museum was even more so. The elegant building behind the band had been open less than three years at the time this photo was taken. What could have been more enjoyable than listening to a little music and perusing the works of art made possible by Edmund Drummond Libbey and his wife, Florence Scott Libbey? *Submitted by Jan Ehrmann.*

LAKESIDE ATTRACTION.

Beginning in 1873, a small community called Lakeside, on the Lake Erie shore, became THE place for recreation and spiritual rejuvenation. Ferries like this one brought families, young adults and entire church groups to Lakeside for educational programs, religious retreats or just a day on the beach. This ferry arrived jam-packed in 1915, with a couple of passengers jumping ship as it docked. People still flock to Lakeside for the same focus on personal and cultural enrichment. *Submitted by Martha's daughter-in-law, Lois Haberstock.*

"LEMONADE LUCY."

As Cedar Point was gaining fame for its midway amusements and dance halls, nearby Lakeside was gaining favor for its relaxing environment, seminars and religious conferences. Many Toledoans traveled the 50 miles eastward to Lakeside to rent a cottage by the week, month or season. In this 1915 photo Martha Haberstock soaks up the sun on the beach, a big part of Lakeside's attraction. Another part was its freedom from the distractions of alcohol and tobacco, which made Lakeside a favorite retreat for Lucy Webb Hayes, nick-named "Lemonade Lucy," wife of Ohio native and U.S. President Rutherford B. Hayes. *Submitted by Martha's daughter-in-law, Lois Haberstock.*

FEATURED IN *THE BLADE,* 1902.

This circa 1915 photograph of the Bihl home in East Toledo is reminiscent of a more genteel era of wide front porches, quieter streets and carriage houses. This classic late-Queen Anne home with its distinctive Palladian windows in the gables was featured in *The Blade* as it was being constructed in September 1902. Built by Joseph and Mary Bihl, the home remained in the family until 1991. The carriage house in back is now gone, but the home at St. Louis Street and Greenwood Avenue is still beautifully maintained by its current owners. *Submitted by Larry Michaels.*

FOUR-LEGGED TEAMSTER.

Earl W. Potts was born in 1882 and was 33 years old when this picture was taken in 1915. A teamster working for the Department of Streets, he poses with one of the horses housed in the City of Toledo Horse Barn behind him. Earl worked for the city until 1952, retiring at the age of 70. *Submitted by Earl's son, Melvin Potts.*

MAIN AND STARR.

Gottfried (Fritz) Wetli had a brick structure built at 652 Main St. and Starr Avenue and opened the Wetli Saloon and Restaurant. The Wetli family lived in the frame house at 648 Main, across Starr from the No. 6 fire station. In 1915, when the Cherry Street Bridge was built, the city knew that, with more automobiles on the road, the zigzag intersection here at Main and Starr would be trouble. The solution: the zigzag – and the Wetli home – had to go. *Submitted by grandson Joseph Wetli.*

THE BARMAN'S REFUGE.

Henry J. Artz tended bar at various saloons in Toledo, including one owned by John Trier in 1900 at 1216 Collingwood Blvd. and another owned by Anton Holzmann in 1904 at 105 Monroe St. Frank X. Holzmann also bartended there and by 1913, Henry and Frank had their own saloon called Holzmann & Artz at 611 Monroe St. This photo shows the living quarters upstairs from the saloon, where Henry and his family lived. It is indicative of the furniture styles of that time. *Submitted by Henry's grandson, Richard Bond.*

CAN'T WAIT TO PLAY.

It looks like the neighborhood children have gathered on a chilly day in 1916 at the home of Thomas Murphy, 3172 Cherry St., to jump rope. Helen Murphy, fur-collared at the center, is trying to free her rope from under a friend's foot.

She is the daughter of Dr. John T. Murphy, who will become the city's health commissioner as she grows up. The doctor and his family lived in his parents' home during his early years of setting up practice. *Submitted by Helen's daughter, Beverly Jackson.*

QUIET EVENING AT HOME.

It is 1916 and the leading news story is the invasion of Mexico and Pershing's order to capture the Mexican revolutionary Francisco "Pancho" Villa. In the small parlor at 1264 Palmwood Ave., Alfred Brower (far left), a tallyman for New York Central Railroad, reads the first section of *The Blade* while his wife, Ida, enjoys a magazine. Their son Jay (far right) sits between the gas-fueled pot-bellied stove, and a boarder, Harry Greiner, who was petting Nick, the family dog. *Submitted by Jay's great-niece, Jeanne Weckerlin.*

PUTTING THE CART UNDER THE HORSE.

Trixie was a special delivery indeed. Believed to be the first horse ever shipped via Wells Fargo Express, the animal traveled from Sulphur Springs, Arkansas, to Charles Schifferd's home in Luckey, Ohio, in 1917. Charles's daughter, Goldie Schifferd, was 12 years old when the steed road into town in style. *Submitted by Joanne Colby, daughter of Goldie (Schifferd) Colby.*

TRAFFIC CONTROL.

As the city grew, and more and more automobiles took to the streets of downtown Toledo in the early 1900s, there came a need for increased traffic control. Police officers had to be stationed full-time directing traffic at busy intersections. George R. Casey is the man in blue at the intersection of Madison Avenue and Superior Street circa 1917. Notice the small platform on which he is standing and the device in his left hand that had to be rotated manually to stop traffic. It wasn't until 1920 in downtown Detroit that the first automatic, four-way, three-color traffic light was installed. *Submitted by Chris Harrigan, great-niece of George Casey.*

RALLY ROUND THE FLAG.

Morgan's General Store on Fearing Boulevard and Wayne Street (now Airport Highway) was a popular stop for cigars, tobacco and confections in 1917. It was believed to have also been a stop on the local trolley line. If so, two of the store's patrons await its arrival. On the front windows, the Morgan's store displays its patriotism in the form of World War I recruitment posters. The top one reads: "Rally Round the Flag. Your Country Needs You. Now's the Time." *Submitted by Virginia Keaton from the estates of Charles and Paul Morgan.*

CLASS IS IN SESSION.

Father Anthony Pirnat pauses his lesson to pose with the youngsters in this 1917 classroom photo. Father Pirnat served as resident pastor of Holy Rosary Slovak Church, organized in the early part of the twentieth century to serve the Slovak people of East Toledo, and taught at the parish school between 1916 and 1917. The church merged with the East Side's St. Ignatius on July 25, 1918, to form Holy Rosary Catholic Church. The two churches were united to prevent St. Ignatius from declaring bankruptcy over years of mounting debt. Among the students in this picture are nine-year-olds Gladys Bongratz (second student, second row) and Amelia Noel (last student, second row). *Submitted by Shelly Piscopo, daughter of Amelia Noel.*

WALKING AT WALBRIDGE.

In addition to the rides and entertainment, beautiful views of the Maumee River made Walbridge Amusement Park a very popular weekend destination for many Toledoans, including Ella Rees and her family. For those who wanted quiet moments, Sundays were ideal for a stroll along the river in the afternoon. In this 1917 photo, Ella stops to rest during a Sunday stroll as she crosses the bridge at the base of Glendale Boulevard and Broadway in South Toledo. *Submitted by Ella's son, Tom Rees.*

DRIVEN TO SUCCEED.

It would appear from this 1917 photo that George Schumann Grocer made deliveries from its establishment on 1401 Western Avenue. Owner George Schumann poses proudly to the right of his truck, with associate Elmer Schultz to the left. The woman and baby on board are unknown. *Submitted by David Newburg.*

AT YOUR SERVICE.

The market at Summit and Cherry streets opened in 1917 and became the shopping focus for most people who lived within the Toledo city limits. The trolley lines all stopped there, where people shopped at 40 different vendors for fresh produce and meats, teas, butter, cheeses, seafood, beverages and fine cigars. The market also had music stores, including one for Okeh Records, one of the first labels to record and market popular music by black musicians. In this photo, the lunch counter staff, including Della Kersten (center), has gathered for the day's work as a customer checks on the baby in the pram. *Submitted by Della's granddaughter, Tonita Strohscher.*

HOMELAND DEFENSE.

Many Americans felt strongly about the war taking place overseas in 1917. By April 6, the United States had declared war on Germany, and its first troops arrived in France less than two months later on May 26. Caught up in the World War I furor, four-year-old John W. LaFrance mans a homemade anti-aircraft gun to defend his family's hearth and home on Islington Avenue.
Submitted by Christine Vischer, daughter of John W. LeFrance

JOHN W. LAFRANCE, HOME DEFENSE
ANTI-AIRCRAFT GUNNER, 1917

TOILET GOODS DEPT.
M. F. NEWCOMER & SON
STORE No 3.

GLASS WITH CLASS.

It's hard to imagine any beauty aid of the time, from toilet soaps to toilet waters, that could not be found at M. F. Newcomer & Son drug stores. Newcomer & Son ran a chain of several drug stores in Toledo at 319 Summit, 701-703 Summit, St. Clair and Adams, 618 Front and 109 Main Street. Store No. 3 was probably the one at St. Clair and Adams. Hazel Redd (left), Lillian Conrad Gregg (center), and an unknown clerk are seen in this 1918 photograph. The stores were all gone by the mid-1920s. *Submitted by Joanne Dearth.*

THE HEART OF MERCY.

In 1918 when this photo was taken, Mercy Hospital consisted of a single building with a 100-bed capacity. Today, its mission of mercy lives on in the medical college and facilities that bear its name: Mercy College of Northwest Ohio, Mercy Children's Hospital, St. Vincent Mercy Medical Center, St. Anne Mercy Hospital and St. Charles Mercy Hospital. Built by the Sisters of Mercy early in the 20th Century, the hospital's front entrance faced Madison Avenue, as shown in this photo. A group of unknown nurses graces the lawn. *Submitted by Mercy College of Northwest Ohio.*

EXPANDING WITH THE TIMES.

In 1889, Fred's brother, Henry, joined him in the family business, opening a grocery store across the street from the feed-and-flour facility. Then in the early 1900s, the family tore down the original wooden building and replaced it with the brick structure shown here. Henry Titgemeier stands to the left of the horse-drawn delivery wagon. His son, Harry, handles the reins. He will inherit the business in 1918. *Submitted by the Titgemeier family.*

READ ALL ABOUT IT!

Gary Schwyn, who lived on Calumet, is the Blade newsboy in this vintage 1918 photograph. The headline is big news about World War I. Notice the well-worn newspaper bag, knickers, and hat the young man is wearing. *Submitted by Barbara Carr.*

A RINGSIDE VIEW.

The 100 degree temperature kept some fans away, but 20,000 people braved the heat for the biggest boxing match in history on July 4, 1919, when William "Jack" Dempsey fought Jess Willard in Toledo for the heavyweight title. Harry Haberstock snapped this ringside photo of the two titans in action as boxing fans look on from the stands. The ring, wood stadium seating, and encampment buildings were constructed at Bay View Park just for the occasion. Jack, the victor, returned to Toledo many times. *Submitted by Harry's daughter-in-law, Lois Haberstock.*

THE GARDEN OF EDEN.

The Reverand Cassius Hettinger, a local optician, began creating these concrete-and-shell sculptures around his home at 1104 Upton Ave. in 1919 after having what he called three "visions." To the elk, giraffe, camel and other statuary seen here, Dr. Hettinger added a caged lion surrounded by statues, scenes from the Bible, and a small chapel. He became an ordained minister of Pentecostal Workers of the World in 1938 and ultimately covered the entire property. His "Garden of Eden" drew visitors from all over the world (as well as the ire of neighbors). It is said that the statues of Adam and Eve crumbled on the day he died in 1955. *Submitted by Dennis Morse.*

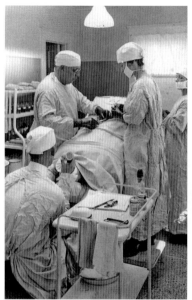

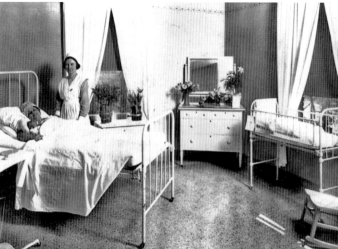

FLOWER HOSPITAL, 1919.

Left to right, clockwise: In 1919, the need for sterile gloves and masks in surgery was still being debated. Note the anesthetist in the foreground using a chloroform drip, the preferred method at the time. Most anesthetists were nurses trained for the task.

If you were born at Flower Hospital in or around 1920, your mother enjoyed the finest accommodations available at the time. New mothers were expected to wear the standard-issue starched gauze hospital cap.

Nurses – and classroom space – were in great demand in 1919 at the Deaconess Nursing School (soon the Flower Hospital). The city's need for hospital care was exploding and any available space went to patient care. These students would help care for up to 55 patients daily. Within five years that number would nearly triple, and the school would again struggle to find room to teach and house its students.

Stevens W. Flower, a successful businessman, and his wife, Ellen, were impressed by the charitable work accomplished at the Deaconess Home, a small private hospital nearby. The Flowers had no children, so when Ellen died in 1903, Stevens made plans to donate the Flower mansion and a sum of money to the Central Ohio Conference of the Methodist Episcopal Church for a new hospital named for his wife. This 1919 photo shows the first three buildings constructed with the Flowers' gifts.

Hilda Ponsler, far left, and fellow nursing students sit for this 1919 photo on the lawn of the Deaconess Hospital nurses' home on Collingwood near Detroit Avenue. As the need for patient beds increased, the nurses' home moved from the Flower mansion to other homes along Collingwood and finally to a four-story school and dormitory designed in 1953. Ellen Hall was demolished in 1955, as hospital administrators began looking for a larger site for the new hospital, now in Sylvania. *All photos submitted by Doris Lewis.*

LOST BEAUTY.

Neither the building nor the vehicles seen in this 1919 photo remain today. The structure, which was the administration building for Willys-Overland, was imploded in 1979. A neo-classical design, it once stood on the north side of Wolcott Blvd. (now Jeep Pkwy.) and was conceived by architects Mills, Rhines, Bellman & Nordhoff in 1915. At the time, Willys-Overland ranked second only to the Ford Motor Company in number of cars produced. When American Motors bought the firm in 1969, the building was demolished to make way for "much needed parking space." *Submitted by Tom Titus, grandson of Willys research engineer, Alvin Keller.*

THE PICKLE LADIES.

The Harbauer Company was a very successful local manufacturer of "cider, vinegar, catsup, pickles mustard and other high-grade condiments" in the early-to-mid 1900s. These ladies are taking a break in 1914 or 1915 at the plant on Harbauer Place from Islington to Libbey, one block west of Lawrence Avenue. The sticks they are brandishing may have been used for sorting or removing blockages from produce chutes. Wanda Kalas (second from left), of 154 Austin St., worked at Harbauer until she married Louis Robaszkiewicz in 1916. The company eventually had three plants in Toledo and was purchased by Hunt Foods in 1948. *Submitted by daughter JoAnn Abele.*

TAKE TWO SELTZERS.

Like its predecessors, this L.M. Hanf drugstore at Broadway and Newbury in South Toledo stocked everything a 1920s family could need to feel and stay healthy. Plus it offered the added luxury of an on-site soda fountain. (See additional photo, page 18.) *Submitted by Rhonda (Hanf) Hayes and family.*

MEAT ON FRONT STREET.

August Jacoby, Sr. founded the Jacoby Grocery & Butcher Shop at 2032 Front Street around the turn of the century. A Hungarian immigrant, he and his sons ran the East Toledo business for many years. It was sold following his death in 1926. August is the mustached gentleman on the right side of the counter next to a freshly butchered turkey. His sons, August Jr. and Alexander, pose in the middle with the store's homemade link sausage. *Submitted by Judy Dorner, granddaughter of August Jacoby, Sr.*

WHO YOU CALLIN' A GREASE MONKEY?

Automobiles have long been serious, big business in Toledo. So, clearly, one could say the same for the city's auto repair shops. Davis Motor Sales' service department at 1211 Monroe Street did a thriving business in the 1920s, as people's passion for the automobile continued to flourish. Years later, upon foreseeing no serious downturn in the auto sales and repair industry, employee Robert Eddy bought the Davis Motor Sales business and renamed it Bob Eddy Buick. *Submitted by Sallie Eddy, granddaughter-in-law of Robert Eddy.*

PROFITABLE RETURN ON INVESTMENT.

On November 16, 1923, Michael Arvanitis purchased a half-partnership in the Interurban Hot Dog cafe' at 450 Superior Street for $350. At the same time, he signed a note promising to pay fifty percent of the restaurant's whopping $700 mortgage. In this photo taken that same year, his partner, Gus Kandis, waits on a customer. Michael was back in Greece fetching his new bride Helen to bring back to the states. His son, Ted, would continue the family's restaurant legacy in later years. His eatery, Theo's, would become a popular fixture on Summit Street in downtown Toledo in the latter half of the 20th century. *Submitted by Michael's son, Ted Arvanitis.*

MILKING IT FOR ALL IT'S WORTH.

Clothed in their work overalls and hair protector caps, these workers from the Page Dairy Company pose at a picnic about 1920. Emma Raitz Clemens, an ice cream packer, is at the right of the back row seated. In the background is probably the Henry Page home on Bronson Place. *Submitted by Judith Lebowsky Shook, a great niece of Emma Raitz Clemens.*

LET'S PULL THE PIN AND ROLL.

Henry J. Bruggeman, the dapper man in the first row to the far right, worked for the Wheeling & Lake Erie Railroad for 42 years, retiring as a car department foreman in 1945. The gentlemen around him are fellow employees. Perhaps it was his experience in supervising tough men like these that gave him the expertise to tackle even greater challenges. In 1927, he ran for City Council of Toledo – and was elected. He represented the 20th Ward on Council until 1934. *Submitted by Henry's granddaughter, Marcia Garner.*

CHEAPER BY THE BARREL?

In the 1920s, the Vischer farm, located on acreage bounded by what is now Sylvania Avenue, Secor Road and Violet Drive, provided produce to a local co-op on a daily basis during the harvest season. Lettuce was packed in barrels to make transport easier and reduce loss of product that might otherwise fall off the back of the truck. Harold Vischer stands on the running board next to an unknown farmhand. Young Harry Vischer is perched on the bumper. Today, St. Anne Mercy Hospital stands on the old farm site. *Submitted by Harry's nephew, Gary Vischer.*

DRUMMING UP BUSINESS.
This local band takes their show on the road via pick-up truck to encourage attendance at a 1921's dance. The sign reads: "Moonlight tonight on steamer City of Toledo. 8:45 sharp. Dancing. Good music." And to prove the point, Albert Nichoson stands up on the back of the truck to wail on his sax. The crowd is gathered on Adams Street near Superior. That's Woolworths on the left behind the crowd. One note: Who will all these men dance with? There's nary a woman in the crowd. *Submitted by Albert's grandson, Norman Nichoson.*

WE'VE GOT CLASS.

St. Anthony's parish closed in the 1960s, but not before hundreds of children were able to take advantage of the education available at its elementary school at the corner of Junction and Nebraska. The students in this first- or second-grade class have donned their best dresses, hair bows, "Sunday" shirts and ties to pose for a class portrait, circa 1920. The blonde-haired boy in the third row, fifth from the left, is Daniel Sydlowski, Sr. – although it would be many years before he would receive or need that title! *Submitted by Daniel's son's, Daniel Sydlowski, Jr.*

MOHR BROS. DELIVERED.

Soda delivery was a lot faster for these drivers in the 1920s, now that they no longer had to use the horse-drawn wagons. Frank Eble, Sr., (far right, behind the wheel) and other drivers are loading up at the docks of the Mohr Bros. Bottling Company at 2516 Lagrange St. Founded in 1902, Mohr Bros. sold soda in 16 wonderful flavors mixed by hand from its own formulas. The company also had a drive-through where you could buy soda in cases of 24 with as many flavors as you wanted. The carriage house for the teams of delivery horses was still there when the company closed in the 1990s. *Submitted by Frank's granddaughter, Betty Szymanski.*

NO BUSINESS LIKE SHOE BUSINESS.
Stanley Pietrzak (right) owned a thriving shoe repair business in 1921. It was a time when people didn't throw away old shoes; they replaced the soles and wore them forever. Then the Depression hit. Repairs were foregone in place of bits of cardboard tucked inside to protect feet from widening holes. Stanley's business closed, and the first floor of 1435 Nebraska Avenue was rented out so he and his family could remain living upstairs. *Submitted by Carolyn Pietrzak.*

COURTING SWEET ALICE.
Immigrants often believed that America's streets were paved with gold, but that certainly didn't apply to Bronson Street, or most streets anywhere for that matter, in 1922. Street paving began later in the '20s as civic leaders became more mindful of the need. Here, John Daczkowski sits at the wheel of his touring car. He is courting the lady at his side, Alice Bugajewski, of 181 Bronson St. Alice's sister Irene holds the family pooch in the back seat. John and Alice later married and ran the Wonder Keg Night Club on Stickney Avenue. *Submitted by John and Alice's granddaughter, Lauren Powers.*

BUILT FOR A LIFETIME.
Proudly stands the Beverly Office of the Swan Creek Lumber & Supply Company at Medford and South Detroit Avenue about 1924. The office had two apartments on the second floor, designed by Ted Althoff, who lived there with his wife, Pauline, from 1935 until 1940 when they purchased their first home at 702 Durango. This building is still in existence. *Submitted by Janet Vogelpohl.*

41

STOCKING THE PANTRY FOR $2.

It's 1925. Celery is 10¢. Red peppers are 2 for 5¢. Cabbage will cost you 4¢ and lettuce, a dime. Want a watermelon? That will set you back a whole quarter. Just ask the staff of Trost's Grocery, shown here on the steps of the store located at Hawley and Campbell. Owner Carl Trost is on the left, his clerk, Edith, (last name unknown) is in the middle, and Carl's son, Walter, poses in knickers on the right. *Submitted by Carl's niece, Carlene Trost.*

ROBINSON FAMILY LEGACY.

Considered by Edward Drummond Libbey to be his best salesman at the New England Glass Works, Jefferson D. Robinson was a soft-spoken leader who went on to become president of the Libbey Glass Manufacturing Company of Toledo. He was also an effective civic leader who helped promote the Toledo Newsboys Association. It was an interest in the welfare of Toledo's youth that was passed on to his son, J.D. Robinson, Jr. The younger Robinson would serve as president of the Toledo Council of the Boy Scouts of America and Toledo Boys Clubs, successor to the Newsboys Association. Both men are shown here in this 1924 photograph, with the elder Robinson holding his grandson, J.D. Robinson III, on his knee. The family's legacy was commemorated in the naming of Robinson Junior High School in their honor. *Submitted by Christine Mather Bothe, daughter, granddaughter, and great granddaughter.*

VALENTINE THEATRE HOTTIES.

The Tunetinker Lassies, an all-female band, performed regularly in Toledo in the 1920s. They are shown here on what appears to be the stage of the old Valentine Theatre, circa 1926. Ruth Gifford (Postal), fourth from the right, played piano. She remained with the band after her marriage, departing only after learning she was pregnant with her son. *Submitted by Ruth's granddaughter, Sue Postal.*

HIS WORK LIVES ON.

The samples of John McCaffrey's work seen here hanging on the walls of his Cherry Street business are long gone, but examples of his craftsmanship live on in many of Toledo's historic landmarks. The McCaffrey Ornamental Plastering Company created the fanciful carvings in many area buildings, including the State Theater and on the ceiling of Holy Rosary Cathedral. He is seated in this 1926 photo fourth from the left behind the wooden grillwork. To his left sits James Ambrose Collins who, along with William Dunlap, would purchase the company from McCaffrey and keep it operating throughout the Great Depression. They would rename the firm Collins & Dunlap. *Submitted by Norene Collins McCollan, daughter of James Collins.*

43

POWER OVER THE CITY.

Frank Nevitt was behind all the electricity that flowed from the Toledo Edison Company for 22 years. He headed the switchboard that switched the flow of electricity to different areas or turned on the turbines and generators to create electricity. Frank (far left) and his crew, pictured here in 1925, made sure there was enough power to run the trolleys during peak hours, and factories planning to run overtime had to notify his office so there would be enough power. Every day, a crewman would turn the streetlights on or off by switches, based on a schedule that changed each day, predicting the time of sunrise and sunset. *Submitted by Frank's grandson, Oscar Miehls.*

MAN OF MANY TALENTS.

From the time Lawrence Matecki arrived in the U.S. in 1900, he built homes, worked as a contractor, ran two grocery stores (on Broadway near Knapp Stree and at 1604 Monroe St.) and founded the Liberty Stores Company, ran a typewriter store on Lagrange and Dexter Streets, became a real estate agent and notary public, had an insurance business, was active in the Polish community, and helped fellow Polish immigrants learn English and other lessons in his three-room garage to pass their citizenship tests. *Submitted by Lawrence's grandsons, Bob and Larry Matecki.*

A TRULY GRAND OPENING.

Today, scores of people drive past the building without a second glance, but the Sam Davis Company at 1510 Elm Street is full of surprises: marble floors, rococo fireplaces and hand-carved moldings adorn its interior. When it first opened its doors on March 28, 1927, dignitaries, politicos, and neighboring residents flocked inside to admire the décor. The woman on the left, smiling at the camera is Mildred Wiemer. The man located top center wearing a fedora and looking up is Paul Wiemer. The woman to his right, in hat, glasses and fur collar is Lola Wiemer. The Sam Davis Company provided a variety of services, including moving, trucking, storage, coal and wood. *Submitted by Donna Mack, daughter of Mildred Wiemer.*

BAND STANDING.
The Neighborhood House Orchestra poses on the steps of a Vinal Street home in this 1927 photograph. The brainchild of "Mr. Pahl", the music teacher (top right playing the trumpet), the group consisted of budding young musicians from around the East Toledo neighborhood. Wesley Carr, second row from the front on the left, played sax. His brother, Russell Carr, front row, second from the right, played violin. *Submitted by Russell's daughter, Barbara Carr.*

CASTLE ON THE HILL.
This snapshot of Harvard Elementary on River Road was taken in 1928, not long after the beautiful school, known as "the castle on the hill" was built. The photographer was young Emily Hirzel, about 16 years old, who had walked with her sister, Katharine, and a friend all the way from their North End home on Buffalo Street to take pictures of the sights along the way. *Submitted by Barbara Carr, daughter of Katharine and niece of Emily Hirzel.*

TURKEY FEET.
Katharine Hirzel (Carr), Emil Hirzel and neighbor Mabel Sheckler sit at Turkey Foot Rock along the Maumee River in this 1928 snapshot. The girls had walked all the way from their North Toledo home to take pictures along the river. Evidently they got tired from the long journey, because Emil Hirzel drove out to pick them up. This photograph was taken by Mr. Hirzel, whose 1920s automobile can be seen in the background. *Submitted by Barbara Carr, daughter of Katharine Hirzel.*

NOTHING CORNY HERE.

The corn borer threatened to devastate area crops in the 1920s. To help eliminate the pest, the U.S. Department of Agriculture established a corn borer office at 615 Front St. in 1928. Lewis H. Colby and fellow field inspectors take a break from their efforts in what appears to be the office mailroom. Lewis's daughter, Joanne Colby, identifies her father as the man seated on the counter to the far right, attired in a short-sleeved shirt, vest and striped tie. *Submitted by Joanne Colby.*

DISTINGUISHED CLOWNS.

These clowns, some of Toledo's most respected professionals, came to St. Mary's School to play basketball with the eighth grade boys in 1928. Kneeling in front are Joseph Thomas (left), die maker at Electric Auto-Lite, and Thomas J. Sauppe, manager of the Scotch Woolen Mills Co. Standing, from left, are Walter H. Hartung, MD, former Lucas County coroner, soon to be state health director and later director of Toledo's health department; Thomas F. Higgins, MD, named superintendent of the Lucas County Home and Hospital in 1933; Nicholas Seybold, MD; Otto Muhme, MD, staff surgeon at three local hospitals and the Toledo physician for Norfolk & Western Railroad; Joseph J. Acker, owner of the Joseph L. Acker & Son Mortuary; John T. Murphy, MD, local pioneer in aviation and internationally known pioneer in roentgenology (now called radiology); and Louis Effler, MD, surgeon and author, named chief of staff at Mercy Hospital in 1933. *Submitted by Dr. Hartung's granddaughters, Mary Ann Kurtz and Martha Frost.*

WHAT GOES UP...

In 1928, a family friend of the Pitzen family built a flying machine in their barn. There was one small setback. The wings had to be removed to get it out. Then there was a second setback. It had to be towed to an airstrip at Detroit and Glendale when the family's 17 acres of farmland proved too rugged for takeoff. Posing with the plane (left to right) are Vera Brown with her hands on the shoulders of Irene Pitzen, Kathleen Fisher and Ceal Pitzen. It's lucky they got this picture when they did. The airplane experienced one final setback: it crashed on its maiden voyage. *Submitted by Rose Pitzen Lemle.*

FULL SERVICE.

George Cornelius was the owner of Cornelius Brothers No. 2, a Sunoco gas station at 3131 Stickney Ave. It was the second station operated by him and his brother, William. The first was located on Starr Avenue. George can be seen here pumping gas from the facility's only pump. His son, Jerry, who took the photo in the late 1920s, remembers living upstairs. The café on the left included a beer garden for evening dining and dancing. It often kept Jerry and the rest of the family awake. Woodward High School is visible behind the station to the right. Cornelius Brothers No. 2 closed in 1942 due to World War II gas rationing. *Submitted by Jerry Cornelius.*

47

ELK CROSSING.

A special group of Elks members, known as the Purple and White Motor Fleet, made a stopover at the Roberts-Toledo Auto Company in downtown Toledo. The year is 1929, mere months before the great stock market crash would affect many of these businessmen, and the Elks, next to their shiny new Studebakers, are part way through their goodwill tour between New York City and Los Angeles. The tour would culminate with the start of the *Elks Magazine* convention on July 8. Trolley tracks, like the ones seen in the lower half of the picture, ran through much of the city. *Submitted by Sallie Eddy, whose father-in-law, Robert Eddy, Jr., and grandfather-in-law, Robert Eddy, Sr., were Elk members.*

AWASH WITH PRIDE.

Taking your clothing to a domestic laundry must have seemed a frivolous luxury during the Great Depression. Such necessary frugality led to the unfortunate demise of many businesses, including this laundry and dry cleaners at 1502 Lagrange St. near Utica. But it is 1929 when this photograph was taken, and times are still good for owners Art and Luella Marx. They pose here with their staff, unaware of the tough times ahead. *Submitted by daughter Doris (Marx) and son-in-law Ed Huber.*

DRIVING ON A DIME.

They pumped your gas, washed your windows, and checked your oil. And they did it all with a smile. For attendants at gas stations across Toledo, that was simply service *de rigueur.* Shell station employee, Leland Goggans, stands just a few feet away from the pump he operated circa 1930. The business was located on North Summit Street near what is now Jamie Farr Park. That year, a gallon of gas could be had for one thin dime. *Submitted by Richard Goggans, son of Leland Goggans.*

PERENNIAL KINDERGARTEN.

In 1929, when these round-faced tots stood out in the cold for this kindergarten photo, DeVeaux area children attended school in portable buildings. That began in 1927, when Longfellow Elementary was overflowing with children and ended (for a time) when the brick school (now DeVeaux Junior High) was dedicated in 1931. It happened again – twice – during and after World War II and twice in the '50s. DeVeaux became a junior high in 1980. That's little Oscar Miehls, front row, second from left. *Submitted by Oscar Miehls.*

THE ORIGINAL STANLEY'S.

Stanley Goscin built and operated this grocery, the original Stanley's Market, at 3303 Stickney Ave. in 1929. Stanley and his wife, Natalie, lived behind the store. By 1934, with the growth of the neighborhood and the explosive increase in prepackaged products, Stanley needed a larger store. So he built it where his customers could easily find him – directly across the street. The store was so popular that when Gene Zychowicz bought it in 1955, he kept the original name. *Submitted by Stanley's great-niece, Lauren Powers.*

DRESSED TO imPRESS.

It's only 1928, but the Dunn family has a head start on recycling. Ten-year-old Beatrice Dunn models a dress her mother made entirely of Toledo News-Bee newspapers to wear in a competition. The frock impressed the judges who awarded Bea with the top prize. *Submitted by Beatrice (Dunn) Rang.*

SUMMER SNOWMAN.

In 1929, Doreen Kamper's family lived next door to the Northwood Villa on Dixie Highway. Her father, Harry, worked at the Villa – which had a few advantages. One warm afternoon he gave Doreen and her friend Luella Lauderman a block of ice to play with. Creativity took over from there. The two girls carved out a snowman in the heart of summer. *Submitted by Luella (Lauderman) Quetschke.*

HAMMING IT UP.

The Tiedtke brothers opened a grocery store in 1893 and it became the first true "supermarket" in the nation. These five gentlemen are probably a fraction of the meat department at Tiedtke's, where this photo was taken around 1930. Mel Fehlberg is second from left, behind the three

men in the foreground. Tiedtke's meat cutters butchered and dressed all poultry and most beef themselves. They ordered hams by the truckload directly from Swift's in Iowa. Part of the butchering staff worked around the clock, just slaughtering chickens, most from one of the poultry farms owned by Tiedtke's. They also sold buffalo steaks. *Submitted by Mel's daughter, Sharon Fuzessy.*

ALL ABOARD!

Otto Knopp sits on the front of this New York Central train engine, his arms crossed and smiling from under his dark fedora. He has reason to smile. He is one of three yard conductors in the Oakdale yards located in East Toledo in the 1930s. He and his surrounding crewmates assemble and transfer hundreds of freight cars each week out of this busy hub, distributing tons of goods throughout the Midwest. *Submitted by Otto's son, Gordon Knopp.*

WHEELS OF TIME.

The City of Toledo Police Department purchased its first motorcycles in 1907 from the Indian Motorcycle Company. Officer Carl Hartung posed for this photo on his Indian outside the police motor barn on Summit Street near Riverside Park. By 1953, the city had replaced two-wheel motorcycles with three-wheel models for safety reasons, and chose to use them exclusively for parades and parking meter duty. This practice continued into the late 1980s. *Submitted by Mary Ann Kurtz and Martha Frost, great nieces of Carl Hartung.*

BUTCHER ON BANCROFT.

Perhaps work was the secret to Fred Villhauer's longevity. Or maybe it was eating his own fresh product every day. In any case, he lived to the ripe old age of 94, putting in 61 years behind the butcher block at the meat shop he ran first at Cherry and Michigan streets, and later on East Bancroft. One salesman recalled in an interview at the time that, "If Fred isn't the oldest active meat dealer in Toledo, he's one of 'em." He is shown on the left in front of his Bancroft Street butcher shop in this circa 1930s photo. His son and assistant, Walter, is on his right. *Submitted by Fred's granddaughter, Mary Candella.*

NUMBERS GUY.

Walking down Madison Avenue near Summit, Rudy Klein looks like he didn't have a care in the world. But this is the early 1930s, after the big stock market crash, and Rudy is chief deputy county auditor. In 1934 he became a tax analyst for the City of Toledo. By 1952 he was serving as city auditor. *Submitted by Rudy's granddaughter, Suzanne Melchior.*

ALL FIRED UP.

Firefighters Charles A. Mortermore (left) and Wallace Gillespie (right) served together at Toledo Fire Station No. 18. But they were more than co-workers. Wallace was married to Charles's sister. Charles served as a fireman for 31 years; Wallace for 50. And he spent every one of those 50 years celebrating New Year's Eve at the station house with his fellow firefighters in case his services were needed. *Submitted by Charles's grandson, Jeff Mortemore.*

STRONG FOR TOLEDO.

Toledo Ice & Coal Co. began in 1929 and planned three new plants in Toledo. Business apparently was good in the early '30s, as this plant and fleet of delivery trucks on Woodruff Avenue shows. The sign on the roofline says, "We're strong for Toledo Ice." That's the influence of Joe Murphy, the company's vice president and co-founder of Citizens Ice Co. in 1906. That same year, Murphy wrote the song "We're Strong for Toledo." In 1909 he organized the Ice House Quartet, which grew to a chorus of 40 or more, toured the U.S. and Europe, and performed at the Chicago World's Fair in 1927. He then returned home and went back into the ice business. *Submitted by Joe's granddaughter, Marilyn McNamee.*

GOOD TIMES ARE BREWING.

Ervin Van Vlerah, on the left, didn't know he was making local history; he was simply a 1930s truck driver. Decades later the Buckeye Brewing Co. would become a Toledo tradition. Here, Ervin poses with another driver, name unknown, in front of the brewery warehouse. Notice the six-digit phone number on the cab – AD 7201 – so different from the 10-digit versions today. *Submitted by Ervin's son, David Van Vlerah.*

STAMP OF EXCELLENCE.

Ralph Dawley worked at City Auto Stamping, circa 1930. Approximately 30 years old at the time, the man's pride in his work is clearly stamped upon his face. *Submitted by Bartha Van Vlerah, daughter of Ralph Dawley.*

JACK OF ALL TRADES, MASTER OF ONE.

By all accounts, James A. Ray enjoyed many fulfilling occupations during his long life: Lucas County deputy clerk of courts, councilman for St. Francis de Sales Church, treasurer of the Knights of Columbus Council No. 386, and deputy clerk of council in the county auditor's office. But it was his skill as a glasscutter that first brought him to Toledo. The artisan can be seen here cutting a vase at the Libbey Glass Co., circa 1930. *Submitted by Ruth Ray, wife of James Ray's grandson, Richard.*

BIG HITTERS.

Toledo has always loved baseball. During the Great Depression, company teams offered recreation and affordable entertainment. Shown is the Electric Auto-Lite baseball team during the 1930s; Larry Rober, Sr., stands in the top row, third from the left, smiling broadly. The Electric Auto-Lite Co. was formed in 1911 with the invention of a push-button electrical starter and lighting system, the "Auto-Liter", for automobiles. Before this, cars had to be cranked to start and headlamps were fueled by pressurized gas lit by a match. By 1937, more than 5,000 Toledoans worked at the Auto-Lite plant, one of its 23 factories. *Submitted by Larry's grandson, Mike Rober.*

QUALITY CONTROL.

The chair in this photo supported not only nine sturdy men, but an entire company. The Toledo Metal Furniture Co. began in 1897 as the Uhl Cycle Emporium on Monroe at 11th Street. Founders Clement, Joseph and Otto Uhl went from making custom bicycle wheels to their own patented household goods. The No. 151 chair, shown here, introduced in 1903 put them on the map. The firm's patented U-shaped construction and unique brace design made their furniture incredibly strong. By the 1930s, they were advertising their extensive line of office products to the nation's "progressive business men" via *The Saturday Evening Post.* As sharp at marketing as they were at design, they expanded or moved five times in just ten years, finally settling in on Hastings Avenue off Dorr Street in 1908. In 1945-46, so many men were off to war that the company had to supplement its workforce with prisoners of war being held at nearby Camp Perry. *Submitted by Marty Uhl, grandson of Clement.*

LOAVES FROM LUTZ'S.

Doris Weckerlin and assistant, Joe Warner, are ready to serve customers in this 1930s promotional photo taken for the supplier of sweets from local Lutz Bakery Co. on Sylvania Avenue. Here's a contrast: the Kool-Aid packaging in front of Mrs. Weckerlin has changed drastically through the years, but the labels on the Pet Milk cans just below her elbow still look the same after all this time. *Submitted by Doris's daughter, Jeanne Weckerlin.*

SOHIO ON CENTENNIAL.

This Sohio station on Centennial at Sylvania-Metamora Road was operated by Frank Knapp (far right) in 1930. In this photo, he is joined by (from left) Nelson Woodward, William Knapp (Frank's son) and Maynard Green. In addition to pumping gasoline (16 cents a gallon), Frank's station doubled as a local store, offering Salada Tea and Kirk's Soap Flakes, among other items. Formerly called the Territorial Road, Sylvania-Metamora was the first road between Toledo and Chicago. *Submitted by Frank's granddaughter, Betty Szymanski.*

MR. SCOTT HIGH.

Austin Hall was a cheerleader at Jessup W. Scott High School in 1931 – and proud of it. He is the young man in the middle, flanked by William Schultz on the left and Jim Kressler on the right. Austin was a University of Michigan cheerleader, too, but for years he returned to S.H.S. to lead cheers at big games. He named his first son Scott and had a grandson named Jessup. Note that in those early years, only young men could be cheerleaders. Young women were known as "pom-pom girls." *Submitted by Austin's son, Todd Hall.*

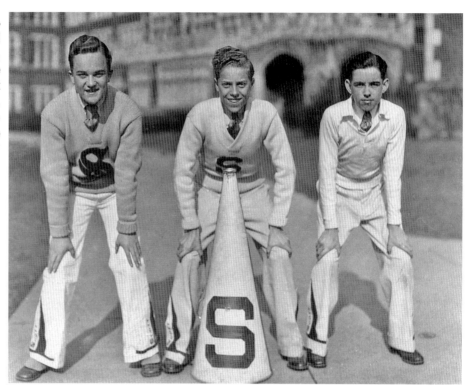

HUNGER HITS HOME.

Long soup lines came to define this country in the 1930s. But perhaps nowhere did the Great Depression hit harder than right here in Toledo, which experienced the greatest banking collapse of any city in America. Across the street from the Ann Arbor Railroad train station, a rail constructed in 1895 as a north-south route from Toledo to Ann Arbor and up into northern Michigan, gentlemen waited patiently outside the Terminal Building on Cherry Street. Out of compassion for those down on their luck Addison Q. Thacher provided dinners on New Year's Day, 1931, at no charge. Unfortunately, the worst was yet to come. By 1933, upwards of 60 to 80 percent of Toledo's labor force would be unemployed, compelling some 60,000 residents to turn to the city for food. *Submitted by Iris Trzcinski.*

57

DRESSED FOR THE MESS.

The emergence of one industry spawns others. As automobiles grew more and more prevalent, spin-off businesses such as drive-up car washes grew, too. The first concept of an assembly-line vehicle wash system, called "The Automobile Laundry", was developed in Detroit in 1914. Manpower pushed vehicles from one cleaning area to another. By the time this photo was taken in the early 1930s, however, a chain-driven pulley system performed most of the hard labor. Still, Doc West is dressed for the mess in high rubber boots and rolled-up sleeves, as he takes a break at an East Toledo car wash. *Submitted by Doc's daughter, Marnette Cunningham.*

HI-SPEED SERVICE.

Franz Norton, pictured in cameo, was the owner of this Hi-Speed service station at the corner of Haverhill Drive and Berdan Avenue in this 1932 advertising card. It was a large station for that era, featuring four bays and offering various services and items such as batteries and tires. Attendants appeared eager to help pump gas or check under the hood. *Submitted by Esther Bevington, daughter of Franz Norton.*

BUSY BEE BAR-B-Q.

Pictured, left to right, are Constance Gregg, Emmit King and Maude King, all ready to wait on customers at the Busy Bee Bar-B-Q. The restaurant was on the corner of South Avenue and Broadway at the time of this photograph, taken about 1932. It remained in business for seven or eight years. *Submitted by Joanne Dearth, niece of Constance Gregg and granddaughter of Emmit and Maude King.*

MARIAN AND MALT ON MADISON.

Before Marian Abelowitz married Irving Odesky, she was a bookkeeper at the Stone Malt Co. at 919 Madison Ave. Today, that would be across Madison Avenue from the Main Library. In this 1932 photo, Marian is nearly dwarfed by the cartons of products. The gentleman may be the owner, J. D. Stone. Stone Malt Co. supplied fountain products to the area malt shops. It closed soon after this photo was taken; many businesses suffered as a result of the Great Depression. But Marian had skills; the following year she was bookkeeper for the Central Tea Co. at 716 Superior St. *Submitted by Marian's son, Stan Odesky.*

READY TO ROLL.

The three Rs have been extended to five: readin', 'ritin', 'rithmetic and rail ridin'. Or so it would seem in 1932 for this kindergarten class at South Street School. On board and ready to roll out of the station are, from left: Jack (last name unknown), Phillip Musgrave, Joe Ann Ryle, Patricia Kirkman and James Gormley. Waiting patiently in line with ticket in hand are, from left: Richard Stowl, Robert Marcey, JoAnna Evans, Leonard Doherty, Norma Jean (last name unknown), Shirley Raitz and Lillian Babcock. The ticket seller is Frances Chorini, and to her left is Marjorie Nochood. The school existed at 867 South Ave. until 1934, at which time its doors were closed and the Lucas County Relief Administration took up residency. *Submitted by Cynthia Rockwell, daughter of Joe Ann Ryle.*

CHARLES AND BESSIE.

Before we had to drive to the supermarket for that head of lettuce, produce and other grocery items were often delivered right to your front door. Charles Abdo and "Bessie" are busy making rounds, which included this stop in 1933 at 824 Bush St. Charles, a Syrian immigrant who came to Toledo in 1920, and son, Lewis, would arrive at the local market at around 3 a.m. to load their wagon with fresh fruits and vegetables before venturing out through North and East Toledo. *Submitted by Lewis Abdo.*

DRESSED TO THE NINES AT 449.

In this June 1934 snapshot, Harry Mee, dressed to the nines, stands proudly in front of a new roadster. The picture was taken in front of 449 Langdon Street in South Toledo. Note the brick paving and the traffic in the background. *Submitted by Joanne Dearth, cousin of Harry Mee.*

LOTS AT WAITE TO CELEBRATE.

The 1934 graduating class of Waite High School stands facing the front of the school for a Tiedtke's photographer. It was a great year: the Waite Indians (changed from "Golden Tornadoes" in 1932) were the city's champion football team. The school, designed by David L. Stine, architect for several mansions in the Old West End, was celebrating its 20th anniversary. And it had a magnificent new, completely walled stadium, one of only three in the state. The homes along East Broadway and the smokestacks of the Edison steam plant are seen in the background. *Submitted by Stephen Makovic.*

61

WONDERFUL WONDER KEG.

John Daczkowski turned the original Stanley's Market at 3303 Stickney Ave. into the Wonder Keg Nite Club in 1934. It became a popular stop for men who worked at nearby factories. At the center of a huge Polish Catholic community, its Friday night fish fry was legendary. John and his wife, Alice, had two daughters: Virginia, seen here in front of the tavern, and Mary. John and Alice ran the tavern until his death in 1957. By then, young Virginia had married Floyd Chapman, who helped Alice keep the Wonder Keg going until 1969. *Submitted by Virginia and Floyd's daughter, Lauren Powers.*

ALL IN THE FAMILY.

Fry is arguably one of the best-known names in local heating and air conditioning services. The Fry Furnace Co., founded by Euclid Fry in 1930, began operation in this building at 2222 Ashland Ave., while Euclid and his family lived upstairs. When his three sons, Robert, Richard and Edward, took over the business in the 1950s, the name was changed to Fry Brothers and the firm moved to 1940 Tremainsville Rd. Seventy-seven years later, the company has evolved again. "Brothers" has been dropped from the name to reflect a third generation of Frys at the helm. *Submitted by Tom Fry, grandson of Euclid Fry.*

GOOD YEARS, GOOD TIRES.

In the first 20 years of the 1900s, Cherry Street was an ideal business location. Benjamin J. Geiger opened a tire store at 1209 Cherry St. after serving during World War I and became one of Goodyear's first distributors. The company name soon changed to Capital Tire, and by 1935 had several uniformed servicemen on staff, including Bob Murphy (left). Capital Tire is still at that address today, with 20 additional locations in Ohio, Michigan and Indiana. *Submitted by Bob's cousin, Marilyn McNamee.*

LOYAL AT LASALLES.

The LaSalle & Koch Department Store stood at Adams and Huron streets for over half a century, and was one of the area's leading retailers. Satisfied customers – and equally satisfied employees – remained loyal to the establishment for decades. Shown is the LaSalle & Koch billing department, circa 1935. Near the windows, fourth from the front, sits Eunice Rock. In May of 1957 she and four other LaSalle employees would be honored with a pin for 25 years of service, presented at a VIP dinner in the Parklane Ballroom. At the time, 115 LaSalle & Koch staffers would also attend. Each had already achieved the same quarter-century status. *Submitted by Eunice's granddaughter, Shirley Pawlowski.*

EASY RIDER.

It's easy to see why Beatrice Dunn fell for Donald Rang. In 1935, when this photo was taken, Donnie was a dashing young man on his riding machine. He stopped to fill the tank for mere pennies at Red Reinemeyer's Sunoco on the corner of Alexis and Telegraph roads before meeting Bea for a date. The couple would be married four years later in 1939. *Submitted by Bea Dunn Rang.*

GO WELL. GO SHELL.

Service stations like this Shell at Dorr Street and Secor Road in West Toledo were typical in 1936. Desperately needed less than a decade prior to accommodate rising automobile ownership and growth of the city, their existence was soon being threatened by the backlash of the Great Depression. Leland Goggans was busy, though. He managed this three-pump Shell station, which was across the street from an AT&T switching station, until the onset of World War II. *Submitted by Richard Goggans, son of Leland Goggans.*

WORKING HERE'S A GAS.

It's hard to imagine, but in October of 1936, this handful of office workers comprised the backbone of the Northwest Ohio Natural Gas Company – and there's more paper on their desks than equipment. Does anyone see a telephone? *Submitted by Chris Kozak of Columbia Gas of Ohio.*

SKIPPING THE 8TH GRADE.

In 1924, Fulton Elementary was the first school in Toledo to be equipped with electric lights. Of course, that was "old hat" by the time these Fulton 7th and 8th graders posed for this photo in 1936. But they were ushering in the next big change, too: theirs was the last class to cover 7th and 8th grades in a single curriculum, "jumping" from 7th grade directly to Jessup W. Scott High School. Among the graduates are Ida Kirk, May Parisky, Edward Eppstein, Shirley Cuthbertson, Thresa [sic] Cutler, Ruth Eshim, Dorothy Davis, Charles Sanzenbacher, Don Steinberg, Catherine Shenofsky, Dorothy Salzman, Arthur MacTaggert, Harold Silverman and, row three, eighth from the right, a smiling Ervine Hening. *Submitted by Ervine (Hening) Frankel.*

65

MARCHING PAST HIS FUTURE.

Carrying a flag, far left, front row, in the May 30, 1936, Decoration Day parade is sailor John T. Miller. As these members of the armed forces march down Monroe Street near Erie, John has no way of knowing he is passing a piece of his future. Eventually he would open his own business, John T. Miller Realty, and he would purchase the building on the far right at 7068 Monroe. *Submitted by Nancy Hardin.*

RUNNING ON BOY POWER.

The only fuel seven-year-old Jim Pennington needed was his brother Don's legs. In this 1936 photo, the two youngsters can be seen cruising along Erie Street on Don's tricycle. Behind them is the Hi–Speed Gas Station, once located on Erie near Galena. *Submitted by Don Pennington.*

BERGER BROTHERS BARRELS IN BOOTH.

Calvin Berger, shown here in 1937 beside a wagonload of freshly picked fruit, hoists a barrel of apples down a shoot for processing into sweet cider. He and his brothers, Frank and Clem, owned Berger Brothers' Cider Mill in Booth, Ohio, just five miles outside East Toledo. Built in 1865, the mill also produced grape juice which, like the cider, was sold in kegs and barrels. *Submitted by Ron Berger.*

FOR ARTS' SAKE.

Workers clear the ice and snow off the Monroe Street steps of The Toledo Museum of Art following a winter storm in 1937. Bill Farm stands upright in the foreground, taking a break to pose for the camera. *Submitted by Donald Brown.*

STANDING ROOM ONLY.

Men's choral groups used to be very popular, especially during the Great Depression. Although minstrel shows had been abandoned to amateurs by 1910, they made a big comeback in 1937 at the benefit performance by the McCune Modern Minstrels, produced by the American Legion Vernon McCune Post #132. It was standing-room only – and that was in the 3,400-seat Paramount Theater. All the performers were members; here the featured performer is Herbert Keeler, with chorus in the background. The proceeds went to civic programs such as the Boys Club, Boys' State camps, the American Red Cross, Toledo Zoological Society, band concerts for hospitalized veterans and the community, books for the Toledo University library, and more. *Submitted by Herbert's son, Jim Keeler.*

THEY'VE BEEN WORKIN' ON THE RAILROAD.

Robert Dearth is pictured third from the right in this July 22, 1937, photograph of day shift workers at the old Chesapeake & Ohio docks. He worked there from 1938 to 1952. *Submitted by Joanne Dearth, daughter-in-law of Robert Dearth.*

WHEN THE "U" WAS NEW.

The original "campus" of Toledo University was a single building located at Cherry and Page streets. In the spring of 1931, however, the educational facility came of age. A full-fledged campus on West Bancroft was opened for public tours. Over 60,000 individuals visited the complex of buildings during a five-day open house. That was equal to one-fifth of the entire population of Toledo at the time. Traffic flooded neighborhood streets as visitors fought for parking spaces so they could walk through the new University Hall and Field House. The buildings were formally dedicated in April of 1931, when Mabel Casey (on the left) and her friend, Harriet, posed outside the Field House for this photo. By 1937, a campaign was on to refer to the campus as The University of Toledo, not TU. *Submitted by Doreen Robideaux, daughter of Mabel (Casey) Robideaux.*

LINE 4, DEPARTMENT 190.

Like many companies of the time, Willys-Overland was hit hard by the Depression. But in February 1936, Federal Judge George P. Hahn granted an order freeing the company from bankruptcy status and new development could once again take place. Restyling and synchromesh brought the Willys 77 up-to-date for 1937 as the Willys Model 37. This photo taken in September 1937 shows employees of Line 4, Department 190 working hard to meet public demand for Willys vehicles. *Submitted by Alice Noonan.*

CIRCUS GROUNDS.

A stretch of land along the north side of Manhattan Boulevard between Lagrange Street and Stickney Avenue was informally dubbed the "Circus Grounds" back in the 1930s. The reason, of course, is visible here. This was where Ringling Brothers planted its Big Top year after year. This circa 1937 photo shows roust-a-bouts putting on the finishing touches before opening day. Today the old circus grounds are home to a residential neighborhood, the new Leverette Junior High School and a shopping center. *Submitted by Delbert Schwab.*

CHALK IT UP TO NERVES.

A lot of talent graced the stage of the downtown Paramount Theater between opening night in 1929 and its demolition in 1965. Barbara Siler recalls vividly seeing the city's own little Theresa Brewer perform *"Ol' Man Mose."* But the performance that probably stands out most in her mind is that of her own. Barbara (far left, in the first row) poses with fellow students of dance instructors Ruth and Eddie Hanf in this photo taken the year of her memorable recital. Wanting to help calm her case of pre-performance jitters, Barbara's grandfather gave her a stick of chewing gum. When Eddie, at the very last minute, instructed the dancers to get rid of their gum, the six-year-old didn't know what to do with it. In a state of panic, she hid it on the roof of her mouth. Unable to concentrate for fear of dropping the gum onstage and getting caught, Barbara completely bungled her routine. Mortified, she cried the entire way home. While Barbara didn't go on to become a professional dancer, the Hanf Studio continues to operate on Sylvania Avenue under the direction of Ruth and Eddie's daughter. *Submitted by Barbara (Henry) Siler.*

A PAGE IN TIME.

The Lagos Market, specializing in Page's milk and butter, opened in 1935 at 1355 East Broadway, near Woodville Road and Vinal Street. One of hundreds of neighborhood markets in Toledo, the Lagos Market was owned by George Lagos, a native of Crete who arrived in the United States at the age of 19. George and his children, George, Jr., Helen, Anna and Mary lived at 1230 Vinal and ran the store for 24 years until George retired in 1959. His daughter, Mary, later established the Toledo branch of the Patricia Stevens Career College and Finishing School. *Both photos submitted by George, Jr.'s son, Tom Lagos.*

CHOCK-FULL AT LAGOS.

George Lagos, Jr. (far left), smiles for the camera from behind the counter at the Lagos Market on Broadway, while his sister, Helen, serves a customer. That's George, Sr., smiling proudly in his butcher's apron and cap. A typical grocery, the Lagos Market was a miniature "supermarket", with a little to a lot of everything from five-cent cigars and fresh-cut meats and vegetables, to boxes of Wheaties for 12 cents a box. George, Jr., was eventually named vice-president. Helen became secretary/treasurer.

SIGNS OF THE TIME.

In this 1938 photo of the Mud Hens, the signs behind them say a lot about life in Toledo at the time. To the far right, soaring above the walls of Swayne Field, is The Toledo Edison marquee, electrically powered, of course, to light up the skies after dark. Printed on top of the scoreboard is the Ohio Citizens Trust logo, a major player in local banking until it was absorbed by competing companies decades later. And visible behind the team, a couple of names still popular today: Kuhlman Fence and Kewpee Hamburgs. *Submitted by Robert Livingston.*

FLOWER POWER.

In 1938, Bill O'Reilly was the head floral designer at Mary Warning Florist. His work – and that of his fellow designers – would have been hard to miss. The company's delivery van made a dramatic statement about the power of Warning's creations. It is seen here making a delivery to Immaculate Conception Church. *Submitted by Jim O'Reilly, son of Bill O'Reilly.*

FROM STABLE TO CABLE.

In the late 1930s, it was a farm owned by George Cousino. Today it's the site of the Buckeye CableSystem towers. Larry Cousino remembers his mother, Laura, taking this picture of his father riding their sulky cultivator through the rows of cabbages, tomatoes, sweet corn and squash. The address then was Rural Route 4, Box 539, Toledo. Years later, it was changed to 5000 Angola Rd., and the only things sprouting there were satellite dishes. *Submitted by Larry Cousino.*

IT'S CALLED MOXIE.

In the mid-1930s, the Atlantic & Pacific Tea Company, better known as the A & P stores, let go a number of employees during labor disputes. One of those employees, meat supervisor John E. Hawley, took it in stride. He opened the H & H Market, 1925 Dorr St. at Montrose, just two doors down from the A & P store that laid him off. Here, in 1939, Hawley stands behind the counter on the left, prepared to beat his competitors at their own game. His partner, Alvin Hogg, is the bespectacled man behind the counter on the right. Possibly the customer was smiling because at that time he could buy bacon by the slab for 23 cents a pound. *Submitted by the shopkeeper's son, John D. Hawley.*

73

NEWSBOYZ II MEN.

The country was still in the thick of The Great Depression when this photo of Hans "Johnny" (left), age eight, and Harold "Tass," age 14, Carstensen was taken in 1939, in the backyard of their home at 1123 Brookley Ave., off Dorr Street near The University of Toledo. To help support the family, the brothers worked as newsboys, delivering *The Blade* in both the Bancroft Hills and Secor Gardens areas. Papers were delivered promptly and to the front door for years, at an average cost of between three and ten cents a paper. For the boys who grew up in hard times, however, life took the road of good fortune. Johnny graduated from DeVilbiss High School, served in the U.S. Navy during the Korean War, obtained a bachelor of science degree from Ohio State University, and then started a successful business in Michigan. Tass earned a degree in medicine from The University of Chicago, after which he joined the Army Reserves and served in an aid station during the Korean War. He practiced in several Army hospitals before retiring after 20 years of service. At this time, Tass went into private practice, going on to pioneer artificial insemination. *Submitted by Lenore (Carstensen) Mortemore, sister of Johnny and Tass Carstensen.*

SMILE! YOU'RE ON CANDID CAMERA.

A roving photographer catches Sue Maher (Dial) and her mother, Myrtle Maher, shopping along Adams Street between Superior and Huron. Note Mom's white gloves – what every well-dressed shopper wore to town in 1939. *Submitted by Sue Dial.*

A COUPLE OF STARS ON STARR.

That's probably "Red" standing in the doorway of Red's Radio Repair shop in this circa 1939 photo. Located at 1007 Starr Ave., his East Side business was a popular service destination at a time when radio was the primary form of home entertainment. It was a mainstay on Starr Avenue for nearly half a century from 1939 to 1987. Next door is another popular East Side destination of the time: Starr Billiards. *Submitted by Henry Frederick.*

ROOM TO EXPAND.

This aerial photograph from the late 1930s shows The University of Toledo campus with University Hall, the old Field House, and the Glass Bowl all visible among the many trees. At that time the campus was as sparse as its student population. The war claimed many students – some who never returned home. Others had to drop out of school due to economic difficulty. *Submitted by Joan Ward.*

GOT GAS?

This 1940s gas company display promoted natural gas as the new and improved energy source for manufacturing companies. More than 2,811,145,000 cubic feet of gas was used locally in 1939 to produce items as varied as stop signs, ratchet sets, birthday cakes and *The Blade* – and that's just industry use. In 1937, 80,000 natural gas customers used more than seven billion cubic feet of gas, and by then all of it was coming from West Virginia. Ohio's fields were all played out. *Submitted by Chris Kozak, Columbia Gas of Ohio.*

STAYING COMPOSED.

Blade employee Erne Scott (forefront) poses with some of his coworkers in this photo from 1940. The men work in the newspaper's composing room, the department that manages typesetting and column layout. Erne worked at *The Blade* for 42 years before retiring in 1963. Son James followed in his father's footsteps and retired from the publication in 1984. *Submitted by Reba (Scott) Harris, daughter of Erne Scott and sister of James.*

GOTTA SEE A GAME.

Actor Joe E. Brown was best known for his comedic role as Jack Lemmon's suitor in the film "Some Like It Hot." He was also an avid baseball player and fan; his dreams of playing major league ball were dashed – twice – by a broken leg. Raised in Toledo, Joe stopped here often to visit his mother on Joffre Street. In 1940 he stopped on his way to a New York gig to discover that he'd missed the Mud Hens season opener, something he rarely missed. He swore he'd find a game while here, and he did. Here he stands with a team sponsored by the Krantz Brewery in Findlay, Ohio. Joe's son, Joseph L. Brown, became general manager of the Pittsburgh Pirates. *Submitted by Betty Printki.*

1940S ENTREPRENEUR.

Phares F. Wing was an enterprising young man. A mechanic at age 32, he worked his way through a number of careers from "Vulcanizer" to used-car salesman before opening his own dealership, P.F. Wing Motor Sales, in 1941. Located at 3815 Upton near Berdan, the business was managed by Phares and his wife Clara, until his death in 1942. Clara continued to manage it independently after his passing. *Submitted by Clara's daughter-in-law, Barbara Wing, and granddaughter, Cary Wing.*

77

TEAMWORK.

Built in 1938 as a WPA project, Toledo Fire Station #23 was located on Central Avenue and Oatis in the Colony shopping area, where it served as a training site. The drill tower behind the station gave rookies hands-on experience in executing ladder rescues from multi-storied buildings. Here, 1940s firefighters scale an unsecured ladder that is being held stationary by fellow teammates holding guide ropes. *Submitted by the Toledo Firefighters Museum.*

MOBILE MARKET.

Like that of the local doctor, it was common practice among early grocery stores to make house calls. In times preceding mass automobile production, the store owner or an employee would load a horse-drawn wagon—commonly referred to as a huckster wagon with fruits and vegetables, cloth and other wares, then drive throughout the community peddling his goods. Often, fresh eggs or homemade butter was given by folks in exchange for their purchases. In later years, these wagons were replaced by trucks, such as the one parked on Waite Avenue near Woodruff in this 1940s photo. *Submitted by Ruth Sturtz.*

IN HIS FATHER'S FOOTSTEPS.

Like his father, Jefferson D. Robinson, Sr., Edward Drummond Libbey's right-hand man, Jefferson D. Robinson, Jr., was also successful in the glass industry. He served as vice-president of Libbey Glass from 1928 to 1935, while his older brother, Joseph, was president. Both sons were well known for their work with the Toledo Newsboys (later the Boy's Club of Toledo). They hosted the annual Christmas dinner for 350 needy boys at the Commodore Perry Hotel, a Newsboy tradition. In 1935, J.D., Jr., established an annual Newsboys award in his father's name for outstanding work in vocational training, a program founded by his father ten years prior. That year, Toledo boys won 27 out of 41 prizes at the Boys Club of America national convention in New York City. J.D. is seen here in 1941 with his wife, Christine (Miller) Robinson, on the patio of their home at 4545 Brookside Drive in Ottawa Hills. He died the following April at age 47. *Both photos submitted by granddaughter Christine Mather Bothe.*

LOOKING TO THE FUTURE.

Photographed in 1941, on the lawn of 4545 Brookside Drive, the Robinson children, Jefferson D., III, Elizabeth Estelle, Joseph, and Christine (Judy) sat for probably the last formal portrait together at this address. The family soon moved to Perrysburg after their father's death the following April. Jefferson D. Robinson, III was 17 at the time and ready to head off to college. He went on to graduate from The University of Toledo and followed his father and grandfather into the glass industry. In 1948, his marriage to Anne Kilbourne Jeffrey would become a major society event; one of his groomsmen was a young, politically minded local fellow named Ludlow Ashley. Estelle went on to marry Rathbun Mather, son of Gordon Mather, founder of the Mather Spring Company, and moved to Princeton, New Jersey. Young Joseph found his true love in Panama while stationed there with the U.S. Army, and Judy became an interior designer in New York and settled in Sarasota, Florida.

ALL DRESSED UP WITH SOMEWHERE TO GO.

The Polish Alliance Group is shown posing by a chartered bus probably in the north end and ready for an outing. The ladies and gentlemen are all sporting fancy hats, handbags, suits, and vests in this 1941 photograph. *Submitted by Joan Ward.*

THINGAMAJIGS AT TIEDTKES.

Featuring every household thingamajig and whatchamacallit you could possibly want, the Gadget Shop, shown here circa 1940s, was just one of the myriad departments customers could browse inside Tiedtke's. From its humble beginnings in 1895 as a modest grocery market at Summit and Monroe Streets, Tiedtke's prospered; relocating in 1910 to the northeast corner of Summit and Adams Streets, where it became the country's first supermarket. The six-story store had a carnival-like atmosphere that entertained as much as it provided goods at reasonable prices. With the addition of restaurants and more departments – a bakery, delicatessen, meats and cheeses, shoes, furniture, hardware, and clothing – Tiedtke's became a shopping mecca. When the business closed in 1972, Toledo said a sad farewell to what was, by then, a civic institution. *Submitted by Jim Fork.*

IN ITS SALAD DAYS.

Edward Wright, Jr., president of the Wright Brothers Greenhouse Company, oversees company employees as they sort and package tomatoes for shipment to the Chicago Exchange in the 1940s. From there, the produce would be distributed to points east. Built on land obtained in a grant from President Andrew Jackson, the 13-acre greenhouse facility was located on W. Bancroft across from the present location of the University of Toledo. By 1956, it was the largest single unit of its kind in the U.S. and the largest single producer of tomatoes, leaf and bibb lettuce in the country. *Submitted by Ed's son, Ed Wright, III.*

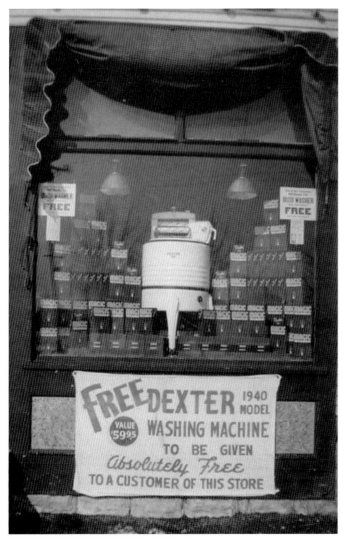

HOT DOG!

West Toledo Hot Dog was a hot spot to grab a seat and a snack in the 1940s. Opened by George Lagos at 4012 Lewis Avenue in 1926, it was a depot for the Short Way bus line, and just steps away from Harry's auto store and the J.C. Penney and Leader's department stores. Officer Frank Mahr (center), a Toledo Police crossing guard for St. Agnes and Longfellow schools, made it a regular haunt too. He is seen here with George's son, Chris Lagos, and an unknown WTHD employee. In later years, Chris would open his own dining establishment, the Seven C's Grill. *Submitted by Katherine Zawodny.*

ARE YOU FEELING LUCKY?

The Weckerlins were just full of great ideas to keep customers coming back. This 1940 storefront promotion offers a free Dexter wringer-washer to some lucky shopper. Valued at $59.95, in a few years it would be worth even more as metals and other materials became scarce because of the war. The next time you're in a Laundromat, check the washers for a Dexter logo; today, Dexter is one of the largest suppliers of commercial front-loaded washers to self-service laundromats in the United States. *Submitted by Jeanne Weckerlin.*

THANKSGIVING TRADITION.

Joe Horvath sweeps right, the football tucked in the bend of his arm, as his Waite High School football team scores a 32 – 0 route over Scott High School, Thanksgiving Day 1942. As quarterback, Joe passed six times during the game, missing the first, but connecting on the next five. For his sports prowess, he would be named to the Waite High School and Birmingham Halls of Fame. Nonetheless, he was not present for his high school graduation. In May of 1943, Joe was drafted into the army, where he would eventually be part of the Allied landing at Anzio, Italy. His mother attended commencements and accepted his diploma in his place – to the cheers of his classmates. *Submitted by Ken Rosenbaum for Joe Horvath.*

GROWING SUPPORT FOR THE WAR.

Homeland support for troops overseas in World War II took many forms. In 1942, Chotty Vergiels and fellow students at Jones Junior High painted slogans on the school's windows encouraging neighbors to do what they could to "Help Them Carry the Load." In this case, homeowners were asked to "Make a Victory Garden." *Submitted by Chotty Vergiels.*

GRAVITY RULES.

Little Janice Wheeler giggles in the background in 1943 as Richard Bond, age 6, shows off his form on metal roller skates with a healthy dose of bravado. His mood literally hits bottom, though, just a few feet away. Richard's mother, Louise, was snapping photos in front of the Bond home at 922 Searles Rd. *Submitted by Richard Bond.*

FULL SERVICE WITH A SMILE.

Long before they specialized in pay-at-the-pump and full-blown convenience stores, service stations offered . . . well, service. Red Head Gas Station manager Henry Harris, clad in spotless uniform, hat and coin changer, stood ready in 1943 to pump your gas, clean your windshield and take your cash payment. When needed, he'd get one of the glass bottles of oil from the stand out front (in background, to right), open your hood and pour it in. Best of all, service was always given while you remain seated in the comfort of your automobile. Even Henry's son Allan, looking on from the doorway of the red-brick building, seemed impressed with the operation. The building still remains on Main Street, just west of Front, in downtown Toledo. *Submitted by Reba Harris, wife of Allan Harris.*

83

I SEE CUSTOMERS WITH DEEP POCKETS.

This is the salon – and possible home – of Madame Mae Frary, circa 1943. The quaint cottage stood on Route 1, Box 94, in Genoa. As a "clairvoyant", we assume Madame Frary chose the location only after gazing into a crystal ball and foreseeing great success. *Submitted by Delbert Schwab.*

LUCKY, LUCKY SERVICEMEN!

Mary Manse College was a Catholic institution of higher education located on Collingwood Blvd. from 1922 to 1975. Run by the Ursuline Order of nuns, it was operated for most of this time as a women's college, before becoming coeducational in 1971. On November 6, 1943, its all-female senior class held a dance in the college gymnasium to salute area servicemen. Rosemary Arvay stands arm-and-arm with a young soldier in the center of the front row. She is the smiling beauty wearing a prim white-collared dress trimmed from neck to hem with buttons. Fellow classmate, Eleanor Lynch stands on the soldier's left. Peaking over Eleanor's right shoulder is another friend, Rosemary Durivage. *Submitted by Rosemary (Arvay) LaVoy.*

DEADLY INTENT.
This Japanese suicide submarine was the rallying point for a World War II war stamps and war bonds event hosted by the Toledo Junior Chamber of Commerce. The rally, which was held in cooperation with the U.S. Treasury Department, Retail Merchants Board, the Toledo Theater Managers Association and local newspaper carriers, took place on July 8, 1943 outside the Melrose and Secor Hotels at Jefferson and Superior Streets. Mayor Lloyd Roulet and Rear Admiral H.G. Taylor of the Civil Engineering Corps of the Navy spoke to the gathered crowd, encouraging their support of the war effort. *Submitted by Delbert Schwab.*

I CAN BE VERY FRIENDLY.

For Verne Strole, right, in the early 40s, they were words to live by. For the Sunoco company some 30 years later, they were words to the national advertising slogan to do business by. Verne owned and operated the L.D. Strole Sunoco station at the corner of Monroe and Upton Streets from 1936 to the early 50s. He acquired a second station in 1940 at Monroe and Detroit Streets, across from Swayne Field. In the 1943 photo below, Verne checks under the hood of a customer's automobile. The Whitney Hills Market, to the right and continuing behind the station, opened in 1933 and was one of the first Churchill's in Toledo. *Submitted by Jennifer Strole, granddaughter of Verne Strole.*

FUTURE FOUNDATIONS FOR STUDENTS.
It is June 1944, and Rosemary Arvay poses proudly next to the sign of her about-to-be alma mater, Mary Manse College. With her Bachelor's Degree soon within her grasp, she will go on to teach mathematics for 27 years at Sherman School and Robinson Junior High. Mary Manse College, formerly located on Collingwood Blvd., educated young adults for many decades before closing its doors in 1975. *Submitted by Rosemary (Arvay) LaVoy.*

WE ALL SCREAM FOR ICE CREAM.
Sixteen-year-old Robert Thorley strikes a fearful pose in this 1944 photo. The life-size polar bear was an ominous landmark in West Toledo, extending patrons a chilly welcome to the Frozen Custard Drive-In located at the intersection of Monroe Street and Sylvania Avenue. In the background over young Robert's shoulder is Ladyfield Catholic School. *Submitted by Robert Thorley.*

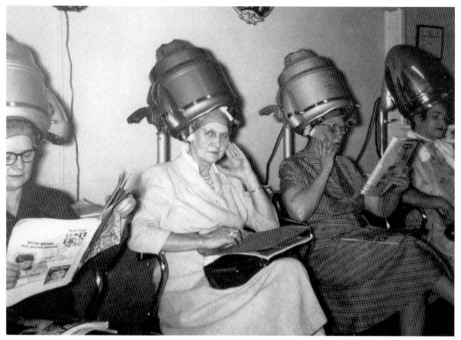

VISITORS FROM MARS?

These ladies are sitting somewhat patiently under these monstrously large hair dryers at the Jenne Wren Beauty Shoppe at 823 Starr Avenue. This photograph was taken in the mid-1940s, not long after the shop opened in 1944. *Submitted by Virginia Hughes, owner of the beauty shop.*

BOXER BUDS.

For 25 years, Lloyd Weckerlin ran a small grocery store and raised a family at Holland-Sylvania and Dulton roads. During World War II, both Lloyd and his neighbor, William Goal, had sons – Harold Weckerlin and Donald Goal – fighting overseas in the U.S. Army. The neighbors made a pact: when the war ended, they would run down Holland-Sylvania Road to Hill Avenue in their underwear. On August 14, 1945, Lloyd (left) and William showed everyone they were as good as their word, and joined millions of war-weary people in joyous and often silly celebrations of the war's end. *Submitted by Lloyd's daughter, Jeanne Weckerlin.*

AGE OF MARKETING.

The shelves are artfully stocked in Hawley's Red & White Market in 1945. Located at 1934-36 Dorr St., the Red & White grocers cooperative provided its member stores with shelving plans that were "scientifically" proven to generate better sales. Note that the Canada Dry ginger ale is strategically located next to the Kuehmann's Potato Chips. Stores also had to use better lighting and more modern, open shelving for better product visibility. Red & White brand products are also prominently exhibited around the store. The age of marketing had arrived.

A famous local brand graces the window of this exterior photo of the store: Shavers Ice Cream. A product of Vroman Foods, founded by local businessman Robert H. Vroman, it was one of many brand delights supplied by a West Toledo plant to thousands of stores around the country. Chilly Things, Santa-shaped ice cream bars and Giant Amazing Banana Thing pops were some of the company's other popular treats. *Submitted by John D. Hawley, son of the store's owner John E. Hawley.*

A GIANT OF A MAN.

Eddie Collins grew up in an orphanage never knowing his actual birth date. Because he believed teenage boys needed guidance and encouragement, Eddie founded and funded baseball, basketball and bowling leagues throughout Toledo from 1923 to 1948 on a maintenance man's salary. Two of his players went on to the majors. The team shown in this photo won their age group's Eddie Collins League championship in 1945. (The team was named for Philadelphia Athletics right-fielder Eddie Collins, Jr., 1939-1942: no relation.) Players from left (in front) are Jack Martin, Ray Mack, Harry O'Neal, one of the Yanksey brothers, an unidentified player, and the other Yanksey brother. Standing, from left, are Dicky Lewis, an unidentified player, Ken Wise, Eddie Collins (with trophy), Sylvester Smith (later All-City selection in baseball and football, 17-year Woodward High School football coach, and Toledo City League Hall of Famer in 1991), and the team manager, whose name is not known. *Submitted by Ray Mack.*

SILLY SOPHIE.

Walbridge Park and its remnants of the old Erie Canal were popular destinations in 1946 – as they continue to be today. Here, the Anaszewicz and Grandowicz girls flirt with disaster at the fall's edge, grabbing a respite from the heat of the day in the canal's cool shade. From left to right they are: Elsie Anaszewicz, Virgie Grandowicz, Gertrude Anaszewicz and Jo, Sophie (straddling the stream), Esther and Evelyn Grandowicz. *Submitted by Pat Anaszewicz.*

NICE AND EASY.

Small trios and quartets were an entertainment staple in area bars and lounges in the 1930s and '40s. Couples enjoyed listening and dancing to the melodic sounds of groups like the Spotlight Trio who played in venues like the Rumpus Room on Consaul (shown here), the Lighthouse Inn, and the Paddock Inn. That's Hap LaLonde on the drums, Norm Laab on the clarinet (he also played sax), and Willie Hunt at the piano. *Submitted by Hap's daughter, Carol (Hap) Cahoo.*

LOST AND FOUND.

Pfc. Walter Markley, on short leave from the service, is all smiles in 1946 as he greets two complete strangers: his sisters, Sally Lou Pieper (left) and Mrs. Harold Miller. The family reunion came about after Walter petitioned the juvenile court for information about his biological family. Court records revealed that after their father died and their mother left home, the Toledo-born siblings were placed into different foster homes. Merely a toddler when his foster parents moved to Akron, Walter had no recollection of those early years. Following the reunion, Walter returned for duty in Washington D.C. *Submitted by Jack Miller, nephew of Pfc. Walter Markley.*

91

SCOOT ON OVER TO SKEETERS.

Dorman "Skeeter" Brumfield and his wife Helen started this open-air fruit and vegetable market at 5001 Lewis Avenue in 1947. Over time, Skeeter added a few essentials so that customers would make his store a one-stop business. First there was bread. Then deli meat. Eventually, he added frozen foods and canned goods. By the late 1950s, the Brumfields had outgrown the open-air building and had built a carry-out in its place. Before it closed its doors for the last time on New Year's Eve, 1970, Skeeter's Market had become a shopping destination for all sorts of items, including beer, wine, soda drinks, flats of flowers, concrete mix – as well as seasonal products such as Easter plants, Halloween pumpkins, Christmas trees and barreled cider during apple-harvest time. *Submitted by Donna Heminger, daughter of Dorman and Helen Brumfield.*

WILLYS-OVERLAND WOMEN.

The 1946 Labor Day Parade was a real celebration. The war was over and the men had returned home to their families. This float by the Willys-Overland Unit of Local 12 won first place and celebrates the women who kept the factories going while the men were at war. The float is pulled by another WWII "hero" – the tough little Jeep. The women on the float are (from left) Henrietta Raszka, Delores Zampkowski, Rosemary Birchard, Bertha Holt and Jeanene Mermer. *Submitted by Bertha Holt.*

DOUBLE DIPPERS.

Sometimes it seemed everyone had a friend or relative who worked at one of the area's Franklin Ice Cream Stores. In this 1946 photo, Leona Gillespie (on the left) waits to scoop a "double" at the Broadway and Western store. The employee on the right is unknown. Chotty Brockway's mother, Golda, and her sisters, Margaret and Jane, worked at this location, too. She would often go to work with them, even though she was too young to be "on the clock." *Submitted by Chotty (Brockway) Vergiels.*

LIVELY LIVE MUSIC.

In decades past, the choice for music at a special event was a live combo such as The Ray Welch Band. A sought-after choice across the country in 1946, the band included guitarist Andy Stifel, violinist Ray Welch, bassist John D. Takas and pianist Elmer Schalitz. Jazz aficionados may recall that John's brother, Bill, was also a well-known accomplished bassist. *Submitted by John D. Takas.*

STUDENTS ON THE AIR.

In 1947, the Toledo Public Schools offered a radio workshop to students considering a career in broadcasting. Under the tutelage of Miss Kellog (first name unknown), juniors and seniors from Scott, Waite, Libby, Woodward and DeVilbiss High Schools spent the first two hours of every school day at Warren School. There they wrote and produced a half-hour radio show. We see the class here on a Saturday morning, preparing to broadcast their show from the studios at WSPD. *Submitted by Suzanne Dennis.*

NO KIDS ALLOWED.

Unable to find someone who would rent their home to a family with children, the Harrigans packed their belongings then gathered the brood and checked into the Plaza. Located on Monroe Street across the Toledo Museum of Art, the Plaza was a combination hotel and apartment complex. The Harrigan siblings (from left), Ed, Charlotte and Bob, pictured near the main entrance of the building in 1947, didn't seem to mind. Young Bob recalls having fun playing in the elevator and sneaking off to the Museum to peek into the art students' classrooms. The Harrigans lived in the landmark building for two years before finding a nice home. The Plaza remained in business until catching fire in the 1970s, after which it was partially restored and converted into senior living quarters. *Submitted by Bob Harrigan.*

ARENA ARRIVAL.

If you lived in Toledo during the last half of the 20th Century, the Toledo Sports Arena was a part of your life. You attended sporting events inside its cavernous hall, saw concerts, received your diploma, shopped for cars, took your children to the circus, cringed at a bull-riding exhibition or cheered a goalie for a great save. It was all things for all events. But, for Marvin Gladieux and his co-workers shown here, those memories were yet to come. They are still busy pouring the concrete for the building's foundation. Marvin is third from the left, standing upright with his hand on the concrete chute. Built for $1 million in 1947, the arena was demolished in the summer of 2007. It would be replaced by a newer state-of-the-art venue to begin construction in downtown Toledo later that year. *Submitted by Marvin's son and daughter-in-law, William and Virginia Gladieux.*

FROM FRANKLIN AIRPORT TO FRANKLIN PARK.

From 1939 to 1952, private planes like this one flew into and out of Franklin Airport on Talmadge Road. The land was owned by the Franklin Ice Cream & Candy Co. and leased to Franklin Airport, Inc. John Aiken, Sr., an aerobatic flyer and airplane mechanic, operated the airport, which had three sod runways and space for 40 planes. It closed because of a shortage of skilled labor for the fixed base operation. These days it's as busy as an international airport, what with 263 stores under one roof, known as Westfield Shoppingtown Franklin Park. *Submitted by Gerald Jacobs.*

THE PAUSE THAT REFRESHES.

This photo shows the Reddish Dodge company picnic at Toledo Beach in 1947. At the left, enjoying his Coca-Cola, is Dick Reddish. The little four-year old boy on the tricycle is Ron Vogelpohl. At right, facing away from the camera, is Kirby Whitty, the general manager at the Shank-Cobley Plymouth dealership, which was located at Adams and 14th Street. *Submitted by Janet Vogelpohl.*

WEIGHING THE BENEFITS OF CREDIT.

At age 17, Edmund Rutkowski was the youngest individual to ever manage a Kroger store, supervising the chain's Superior Street location for a number of years before opening his own establishment. He is seen in this June 1947 photo weighing a customer's purchase at his store on Lagrange and Noble. His brother-in-law, Joe Walczak, is helping out behind the meat counter. Note that though the sign on the wall states, "Please Do Not Ask for Credit," Ed was the employee who ignored this dictum most often. He was known throughout the neighborhood as a man who would extend credit to those in need. *Submitted by Edmund's daughter, Gloria (Rutkowski) Heigel.*

MODEL RAILROAD.

In January 1947, downtown Toledo's waterfront was chugging along, bustling with railroad engines and freight cars. Toledo has evolved into one of the top five rail hubs in the U.S. loading such items as petroleum products, automotive parts, automobiles and food products. The same view today, taken from the high-level bridge, would show the Owens Corning world headquarters and Promenade Park. *Submitted by Gerald Jacobs.*

97

TWO-WHEELIN'.

Emile Thomas snapped this photo in 1948 of her nephew Robert Schaal, proudly displaying his bicycle and some pretty snazzy riding gear. Young Robert was staying with his Aunt "Mille" and Uncle Joe (Benard Thomas) at their home on Locust Street, near Moore Street, while his mother, Loretta Schaal, recovered from illness. *Submitted by Judith Shook, granddaughter of Emile Thomas.*

THANKS FOR EVERYTHING.

In 1945, actor/comedian Bob Hope came to Toledo to visit his brother Sidney, a farmer from Ridgeville Corners who was ill at St. Vincent Hospital. Hope and his four brothers grew up in Cleveland. When Sidney passed away, Hope wanted to show his gratitude for the care his brother received. In 1946, the hospital launched a campaign to raise funds for a major expansion. On May 28, 1947, Hope brought the entire crew of his hit radio show, including Desi Arnaz and his orchestra, and Cleveland Indians' ace pitcher Bob Feller, for a benefit at the Swayne Field ballpark. Despite unseasonably cold weather, the show raised more than $15,000 for the hospital. Here he stands with one of many fans who braved the cold. *Submitted by Alice Verb.*

1948 BC (BEFORE COMPUTERS).

The billing department of LaSalle & Koch Department Store was a pretty cramped and busy place in the late 1940s. Every bill had to be typed by hand and, after 83 years in business, the store had a lot of customers. Those doing the typing along the right wall are (from front) Cora Thomas, Velma Newbirt, Eunice Rock and Virginia Snell. *Submitted by Eunice's granddaughter, Shirley Pawlowski.*

ALL-AMERICAN FLOOR.

In 1925, the American Floor Surfacing Machine Company built this modern brick, steel, and concrete plant on the site of its original building at 518 South St. Clair Street. Roadsters are parked in the lot on the near side of the building, which belonged to the city, in this 1948 photograph. At the left is the view south on St. Clair toward Logan Street. During World War II, the company manufactured and assembled parts for guns, tanks, and planes. In April 1957, the name of the company was changed to American Floor Machine, and became a division of American-Lincoln. It was acquired by a Cleveland company in 1968, and the plant was moved to Bowling Green in 1972. After several other changes of ownership it went out of business in 2005. *Submitted by Marcella DeMars, who worked there for 53 years.*

BORN TO BE WILD.

Bob Meinen, on the left, and Dale Errington, on the right, show off their Whizzer motor bikes. When he put the pedal to the metal, Dale's souped up model could reach speeds of approximately 40 mph. This circa 1948 photo was taken along the 2900 block of Copeland Boulevard facing west. *Submitted by Dale Errington.*

A "GRAND" SPECTACLE.

In years past, a senior prom was a grand and formal event. Here, members of the Macomber High School Class of 1948 take part in a Grand March. Notice the extravagant gowns – and the even more extravagant corsages! *Submitted by Betty Printki.*

WHO'S ON FIRST SHIFT?

Willys-Overland was a popular attraction for out-of-town celebrities visiting Toledo. Charlotte (Bialecki) Sicklebaugh worked in the export department in the 1940s, and saw numerous notables, including Tony Curtis and Janet Leigh. Here she is pictured with the comedy team of Abbott and Costello. Charlotte is in the dark skirt next to Bud Abbott, accepting a hug, while Lou Costello kisses a co-worker. *Submitted by Tim Sicklebaugh.*

FULL OF PUNCH.

Referee and retired Blade employee Louis "Dutch" Mauder casts a keen eye on Cecil Hudson (left) as Tommy Bell throws one his deadly left-hand punches during the November 16, 1948, boxing match at Toledo Sports Arena. The action was captured in this photo by Dwight Boyer, who also worked at The Blade between 1944 and 1954. Despite Hudson's valiant effort, Bell went on to win the match by decision. *Submitted by Naomi Sommers.*

WELL-EARNED WHITE CAP.

It is 1949, and Toledo District Fire Chief Frank O. Carson and his driver, Elvin Casper, stand in front of a 1947 Pontiac fire truck in one of the many stations of which he is in charge. Frank joined the fire department in 1911 and received the white cap of a district chief in 1937. He retired one year after this photo was taken, after 39 years in the department and was rated by Toledo's fire fighters as one of the best-liked command officers in the history of the fire division. *Submitted by Frank's granddaughter, Bev Jackson.*

"SO YOU WANT TO LEAD THE BAND".

That was the name of the contest 12-year-old Bob Krueger entered in 1949. The highly popular audience-participation segment was a

staple feature during performances by legendary bandleader and songwriter Sammy Kaye, standing right of Krueger. Following an interview and vocal rendition of Jingle Bells, the young lad was chosen by Kaye to join two other contestants in trying his hand at conducting during a Christmastime matinee performance at the Paramount Theater on Adams Street. Despite his brave effort and the cheers extended him by his sister, Shirley, Bob didn't win the event. And though he has not since leapt on stage to conduct a band, Krueger cherishes a keepsake from that memorable day: the baton he waived. *Submitted by Bob Krueger.*

SCHOOL READINESS.

The concept of kindergartens was still relatively new to public school systems at the start of the 1940s. But private elementary schools had been quick to adopt the idea of providing "school readiness" training to five-year-olds. Here, the 1947 kindergarten class of St. Phillip's Lutheran School (Indiana and Elizabeth Streets) poses proudly with its teacher, Mrs. Esther Pransche. Marnette Thomas (Cunningham) is the little girl to the far left in the front row. She's dressed to the nines for this happy occasion, wearing a checked dress and knee socks. *Submitted by Marnette Cunningham.*

HUCK FINN, HERE WE COME.

Neighborhood kids like Sue Page and Virginia Guiton called it the Sutter and Chase Marsh – and they delighted in sailing across it on their homemade rafts. Unfortunately for these young sailors, the marsh that was located behind Chase School in 1949 was eventually filled in. *Submitted by Virginia's daughter, Christine Parks Papenfuse.*

GRADUATION DAY.

It's graduation day for the kindergarten class at St. Hedwig School in 1949, and all 46 children are getting a hearty meal, complete with candle centerpiece. Front and center in the striped shirt and dashing two-toned shoes is Larry Rober, Jr. The school began kindergarten classes in 1934. A proud Sister Mary Thomesine and Father Anthony Pietrykowski are featured in the back of the room. *Submitted by Larry's son, Mike Rober.*

A REEEEEEEALLY BIG DEAL.

Ed Sullivan was in Toledo in 1950 for a promotional event, but a paying gig wasn't enough for the entertainment impresario who had a reputation for encouraging young people to follow their dreams. Sullivan asked the event planner to arrange for him to meet a few of Toledo's high school students. Central Catholic High School was the lucky pick. Seated from left to right are Florence LaPorte (Ehrsham), Sue Kelley (Badyna) and Phylis Scheter (Wright). Standing left to right are Fr. Fuqua, Jim O'Shea, Ed Sullivan, Msgr. Harrington, Gerry Howard and David Jagodzinski. *Submitted by Sue (Kelley) Badyna.*

NO SPRINGS. HONEST WEIGHT.

The slogan is synonymous with Toledo Scale Company. Founded in 1901 by Henry Theobald, it fast became the premiere manufacturer of scales of all types and sizes. In later years, Toledo Scale introduced a complete line of modern food machines to their ever-expanding product line, including choppers, mills and slicers. John Hornyak (to the immediate right of the two men in the foreground) works on the assembly line producing food machines in 1958. He retired from Toledo Scale seven years later, after 15 years of service. *Submitted by Cecile Grandowicz, daughter of John Hornyak.*

ACTING ACCORDINGLY.

Before the electric guitar became the most common instrument you bought for your budding musician, it was the accordion. These students of the Trick Brothers Accordion Institute are lined up like sardines in the WSPD studio in 1950 to play live for listeners. Front and center is young Allan Harris. Between him and the giggling girl to his right is his buddy, Chuck Sieving. The sardines seen through the glass are their proud parents. *Submitted by Reba and Allan Harris.*

THE GRANDMOTHER HAS LANDED.

And by the looks of things, she's in for a chilly reception. Jane Hones and her two children, John (left) and Nancy, huddle together for this photo-op in 1950, as they wait for Grandma Edith Truxton to deplane. Her journey has brought her to Toledo Municipal Airport, just east of Toledo, in Millbury, Ohio. Before it was acquired by the City of Toledo in 1936, this airport had been named Toledo Transcontinental. Poor planning in building the first local airport, Stickney Avenue, which opened in 1927, lead to the immediate need for the Millbury location in 1928. *Submitted by Nancy (Hones) McCoy.*

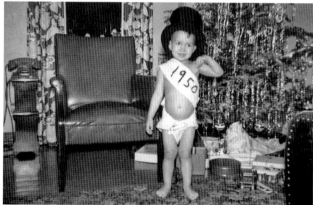

DRESSED FOR THE HOLIDAYS.

Bobby Cairl, Jr. struts his stuff as a 1950 New Year's baby, courtesy of his Aunt Bea. The year 1949 is about to be counted down and out in the living room of her Point Place home on Keen Street. *Submitted by Bea Dunn Rang.*

GONE BUT NOT FORGOTTEN.

Although St. Agnes School is now closed, the memory of its victorious 1950 football team lives on in this photo. The 7th and 8th grade boys had a 7-1 season. Identified players include: Front Row, second from left, Agnes's brother, Warren Miller; third from left, Barney Fackleman; fifth from left, John Hancock; and with hand on bench, Lee Hood. Front Row, first from right, Jack Wise; second from right, Joe Dorm; fourth from right, displaying his St. Agnes jacket, Dave Gladieux; and fifth from right, Ray Hood. Back Row, second from left, Kenny Row; sixth from left, Dick Roschelle; seventh from left, Pat Cassidy; and eighth from left, with arms around players, Coach Jack Shea. Back Row, third from right, Jim Wise. *Submitted by Agnes Miller.*

STAMP ON TOLEDO.

Founded in 1911 by Grafton Acklin and three of his sons, Acklin Stamping Company, then located on Nebraska Ave., contributed greatly to Toledo's rise in prominence in the industrial world. That came largely at the hands of highly skilled and dedicated tradesmen, such as Louis Siler, shown here in the company's die shop in the 1950s. Louis was extremely proud of his work; and Acklin Stamping was deeply appreciative of his many years of service, as was expressed in 1960 with the traditional presentation of a personalized cigarette lighter. Acklin Stamping was purchased in 1999 by ICE Industries and is now located in Sylvania. *Submitted by Barbara Siler, daughter-in-law of Louis Siler.*

PLAY IT AGAIN, TOM.

Drummer Tom Rees played with a lot of musicians over the years. In this 1950 photo, he's performing at Thompson's Inn on Edgewater Drive in Point Place as part of the Joe Sotteck Trio. Joe is playing sax while Don Smyth tickles the ivories. The trio played at a number of venues, including Tony Packo's, the Swan Club, Gulish Villa, the Step Inn and the Northwood Villa on Summit Street, the site of one of Yonnie Licavoli's largest illegal whisky stills. It does business today as Fritz & Alfredo's. *Submitted by Tom Rees.*

PRETTY AS A MAY DAY.

A sunny afternoon, lovely lassies in long dresses, a May pole and a picnic lunch – what could be finer? The Rossford Library hosts a celebration of spring on its lawn in this photo of a May Day festival, circa 1950. *Submitted by Jeannine Wilbarger, Rossford Library.*

TRUE SOHIOANS.

In 1956, Chuck Hickman's Sohio station at the Colony Shopping Center on Central Avenue was one of the busiest and most successful full-serve gas stations in West Toledo. This station alone pumped 70,000 gallons of gasoline a month – that's a lot of S & H green stamps. Chuck obviously had an uncanny sense for choosing ideal locations; he owned other stations at Nesslewood and Detroit avenues and Canton Avenue and Jackson Street downtown. He acquired two more seven years later.

Hickman's Colony Sohio specialized in many different services including transmission work, brakes, mufflers and valve replacement. The station had three service bays, and two of his six employees were seasoned mechanics. Not only did they install mufflers and tailpipes free, they gave S & H green stamps and supported the local economy by installing only AP Parts, made in Toledo.

Just one block off West Central Avenue, you could see a movie at the Colony Theater, bowl at Colony Bowling, buy furniture at Gravelle's, carpet at Richard's Carpets, purchase a suit at Richman Brothers, shoes at King's Shoes, tools at Norton Hardware, toys at Hobby Lobby or dine at Greunke's Cafeteria.

Pictured, lower left is Chuck Hickman, center, with Eugene Jackson (left) and Wayne Sanders, two of the six men who worked there full-time in 1956.
Submitted by Bruce & Bev Hickman.

KING OF THE RAILS.
Marvin Druckemiller stands in front of what could be one of the most recognizable steam engines in the annals of railroading: the "Wabash Cannonball." Old #673 was one of several J1 Pacific 4-6-2 steam locomotives that roared along the rails between Toledo, Ohio, and Fort Wayne, Indiana, piloted by Druckemiller. A railroad engineer for 38 years, he stands proudly next to his "partner" in the Sumner Street Yard, near the DiSalle Bridge (where I-75 crosses the Maumee River), circa 1951. *Submitted by Marvin's son, Bob Druckemiller.*

RAILROADED.
Prior to 1950, automobile traffic along Reynolds Road had to bump over the railroad tracks located near Angola Road. Construction on a railroad overpass began at the site in the 1950s. The views north and south of the project show long expanses of barren land and few buildings – a far cry from the bustling business community found there today. *Submitted by Larry Cousino.*

JAZZED UP.

From the 1920s through the 1940s, Toledo's Waiters & Bellman's Club at 545 Indiana Ave. was the hottest place for live jazz. The club hosted many national acts – Louis Armstrong, Duke Ellington, Count Basie and Andy Kirk all sat at the bar pictured here. Art Tatum, Jr. played there regularly by age 19, often with another Toledoan and future jazz great, Jon Hendricks, then just 14. Jazz musicians – local or traveling, all ethnic backgrounds – came to the Waiters & Bellman's Club for after-hours jam sessions that went well into the morning. By the 1950s, music interests and the club's clientele had changed, and the club drifted into history. *Submitted by Marnette Cunningham.*

THE FIVE POINTS.

This bustling commercial area in 1951 is where Sylvania, Phillips and Lewis avenues come together. It remains one of Toledo's most stable retail "strips," even though the stores seen here no longer exist: Leader Department Store (one of several), Bellman's Market (one of three in town), Start's Drug Store (as in Roy C. Start, pharmacist, two-term Toledo mayor and namesake of Start High School) and Harry's Auto stores. You won't get this open view at the "5 Points" anymore, either. Today there's a traffic-diversion island with a stop light in the roadway. *Submitted by Mary McCartney.*

111

AHOY, MATEY!

Harry Hones received permission to go ashore and have his picture taken by his daughter, Jane, while the ship docked in the Bayshore area to load ore. Between 1954 and 1961, Harry served as a deck hand aboard the *John Hulst*. The 611-foot vessel was among the first ore carriers on the Great Lakes to be equipped with steam turbines for main propulsion. It was also among the first of the fleet to incorporate continuous passage below deck, eliminating the need for crew members to go forward and aft on the spar deck in bad weather. *Submitted by Nancy (Hones) McCoy, daughter of Harry Hones.*

SMILE, YOU'RE ON...

What appears at first as a slice-of-life snapshot is more than likely a professionally designed print advertisement for Toledo-area Buick dealerships. The approach is refreshingly original. No models or celebrity endorsements. No technical diagrams or pie-in-the-sky gibberish. Instead,  the automaker uses ordinary-looking people in the local hometown setting (note Walgreen Drugs and Stein's in the background), enabling readers to envision realistically just how swell it would be to own this vehicle. *Submitted by Sallie Eddy, granddaughter-in-law of Robert Eddy, founder of Bob Eddy Buick.*

TAKING OFF FOR LUNCH.

Everyone likes to get away for lunch, but Community Traction Co. bus drivers David Newburg (left) and co-worker Gayland Orner took things to the extreme back in the 1950s. The two often flew to Port Clinton to eat at the airport restaurant during their lunch breaks. *Submitted by David Newburg.*

FREE SKATING.

Although seven-year-old Nancy Hones took a tumble on the frozen waters of Pearson Park pond, she couldn't help smiling. Winter wouldn't have been the same without this ice-skating mecca. With its much-photographed stone bridge in the background, this 1951 photo could have been taken yesterday. *Submitted by Nancy (Hones) McCoy.*

WHAT A BARGAIN!

In the early 1950s, this Hy-Flash station was selling regular gasoline for 27.9 cents a gallon. The station was at 4654 N. Detroit Avenue, between Sylvania and Lagrange. They also offered motor oil for 20 cents, a three-truck discount and free ice water. However, don't drive over there looking for this great deal, because the station has not been in business since 1981. *Submitted by Randy Studer.*

FATHER OF A MUSICAL MIRACLE.

Art Tatum, Sr., began working in the Foundry National Supply Company in 1926, making him what the firm called a "National Supply man." But he was better known as the father of jazz great Art Tatum, Jr. The company newsletter, the *NASCO News*, featured the senior Tatum in its April 1950 issue, seated at the piano in his home holding a photo of his famous son. Art Tatum, Jr., who taught himself to play the piano at the age of 3, held his last Toledo performance at the Latin Club. He died six years after this photo was published. He received a Grammy Lifetime Achievement Award posthumously and is recognized as one of the greatest jazz musicians of all time. *Submitted by National Supply Company employee Paul Sprouse.*

113

GOING TO THE DOGS.

This aerial view shows the large Kasco Feeds operation at 1352 East Broadway about 1950. Kasco, which survived a devastating fire in the 1930s, made primarily dog food. During its last years, it was known as Worthmore Feeds, and the plant was dismantled by the late 1950s. The buildings on East Broadway at the lower left of this photo still exist, as do the houses at the upper right on Kedron Street. *Submitted by Alice Verb, who worked at Kasco during World War II.*

THE POWER OF MARKETING.

It takes more than a quality product to be a successful company. It takes marketing. In the 1950s, the Sun Oil Company, now Sunoco, was well invested in public relations. These photographers were all employees of Sun, hired specifically to record and communicate the company's activities to the world. John Verb, kneeling coatless at the right end of the front row, worked for the company for 25 years. Robert Packo, son of noted restaurateur Tony Packo, is first on the left in the top row, wearing a dark sweater. *Submitted by Alice Verb, wife of John Verb.*

RECOGNIZE THIS BUSY STREET?

The church to the left in this circa 1950 photo may look familiar. It's the Olivet Lutheran Church at 5840 Monroe St. Still can't place the location? Imagine the Dave White car dealership in place of George Gindele's Mobile Home Sales. Owned by George and his wife, Clara, it was considered a rural retail location at the time. Today this strip of Monroe where it intersects Alexis Road is one of the area's busiest intersections. *Submitted by Clara's daughter-in-law, Barbara Wing, and granddaughter, Cary Wing.*

SAMMY SELLS.

Promotions, like the ones featured in this window in 1951, helped small businesses sell their products and services for many years. Here, a Sammy Kaye concert sponsored by Sylvania Television drives potential customers into Bayes Electric to pick up free tickets. Bayes Electric was founded in 1937 and closed in 1956, five years after this photo was taken. It offered televisions, radios and other electronics for sale, along with repair services. *Submitted by the owner's son, Jim Bayes.*

115

HOME SHOW SHOWOFFS.

Bayes Electrical Appliances had a prominent booth at the Annual Home Show in the Toledo Civic Center in 1951. Jim Bayes stands behind the latest model television from Admiral – a hot new item in the early '50s. Bill and Mary Bayes hold down posts near the refrigerators and freezers, prepared to boast the products' many benefits. Bayes Electric was operated at 309 Main St. until 1956. *Submitted by Jim's son, Jim Bayes.*

LOOK, MA – ONE HAND.

Marcella Moorehead DeMars, who worked for the American Floor Surfacing Machine Co. as a clerk in the purchasing department, also doubled as a model demonstrating the new portable machinery in this 1951 photograph. She worked for the company for over 53 years, beginning on April Fool's Day in 1946. *Submitted by Marcella Moorehead DeMars.*

A LITTLE OFF THE TOP.

The Gaylords Barbershop Quartet brought sweet music to the ears of many Northwest Ohioans in the '40s and '50s. Although no one can say for certain exactly when barbershop music began, the style of *a cappella* comprising four-part harmonies and ringing chords is a uniquely American folk art. After broadcasting for years on radio, their performances, like this one in 1951, were seen on WSPD-TV. Pictured are, from left, Virgil Henry on guitar, Marv Stimphly, Joe Bauer and Al Gause. *Submitted by Barbara (Henry) Siler, daughter of Virgil Henry.*

BEFORE THE TROTTERS.

Before harness racing took off at Raceway Park, the track was a popular site for automobile racing. Here the ladies line up to tackle the oval in the park's Powder Puff Races, circa 1951. *Submitted by Shirley Pawlinski.*

GUARD ON DUTY.

To see anyone in the 107 Building at Willys-Overland Motors on North Cove Boulevard in December 1952, you had to get past Security Guard Eddie Heiss. Heiss provided clearance for all visitors who arrived to meet with engineers and factory office people on the second floor. On the right is typist Phyllis Hood from the Tool Engineering Department. The company celebrated making the millionth Jeep in March of 1952. But this was to be their last Christmas working for Willys-Overland; the company was sold to Kaiser-Frazer in 1953. *Submitted by Ruth Marquart.*

INSURING FAIR NEGOTIATIONS.

When the agents of Makovic Insurance, 1807 Milroy St., went on strike against Prudential in 1952, the agency's owner, George A. Makovic, was right beside them. Seen second from the left, George played football for Waite High School in the early 1930s, graduated from WHS in 1933, worked for the USO before enlisting in the Marines and eventually served as Toledo's recreation division supervisor. *Submitted by Stephen Makovic, son of George A. Makovic.*

WHEN HE WAS JUST TOM.

Patricia Rudes is seated at center, facing Jim Liedtke, in this December 1952 production of "The Madwoman of Chaillot" performed at BGSU's Gate Theater. Seated second from the left is freshman student Tom Conway, who went on to become Tim Conway of *The Carol Burnett Show*. Tom Chestnutwood is at far right. Pat Rudes was a grad student at the time who also performed plays in Sidney, Huron, Waterville, BGSU and the Toledo Repertoire Theatre. *Submitted by Pat Rudes.*

BAT BOY FIRST.

The Commodores, a Perrysburg baseball team, is pictured in this 1952 photograph. They played in the Toledo Federation Baseball League at Perrysburg High School. In 1954 the team name was changed to the Perrysburg Merchants. Frank Pinciotti, who played outfield and first base, is in the front row, third from the left. The bat boy is none other than Jim Leyland, the current manager of the Detroit Tigers. *Submitted by Frank Pinciotti.*

ENGINEER OF CHANGE.

One consulting engineer in the late '40s and early '50s did more to change the face of Toledo than any other: Porter W. McDonnell. For years connected with the Toledo and Lucas County plan commissions, he was appointed city services director in 1949. It was his consulting engineering firm that oversaw development of the area's first shopping center on a 60-acre site at the southwest corner of Jackman and Laskey roads: the ten-million-dollar then-named "Town & Country Miracle Mile." *Submitted by Porter's daughter, Jean (McDonnell) Wagoner.*

STRUCTURED.

The bridge that marks the entrance to the Owens Corning headquarters at Washington and Summit streets today mirrors one that stood there decades before. The original structure was dismantled in the early '50s. Elwyn Newburg worked at Spicer then, but picked up excavating work during layoffs. He is seen on the right dismantling the operator shed roof next to fellow worker Burt Delmont. *Submitted by David Newburg, son of Elwyn Newburg.*

WAGONERS.

Where else would you expect to find the Wagoner kids but . . . well, in a wagon. Robert, Virginia and Mari Lynn take in the sights along Commonwealth Avenue, east of Jackman Road, in 1952, seated comfortably in the pride and joy of every girl and boy – a red Radio Flyer wagon. An icon of Americana, Radio Flyer was named after designer Antonio Pasin's fascination with fellow Italian inventor Guglielmo Marconi's brainchild, the radio, and his fascination with flight. *Submitted by Virginia Wagoner.*

SCHUMANNNN?

A wrecker removes a car from an accident in front of Schuman's Market at Western Avenue and Spencer Street in 1953. Note the evolution of the store's name. The sign protruding from the corner of the building features the owner's name as it was spelled in 1917. The sign above the door shows it with only one "n". *Submitted by David Newburg.*

SWEET AS CAN BE.

A young Sandra Drabik purchases a sweet treat from a Penguin Ice Cream vendor working his way down Foster Drive in 1953. Peddle-powered ice cream carts traversed many neighborhood streets in the 1950s. Filled with heavy quantities of ice and product, vendors needed strong legs and stamina to make it through a long summer day. But If you were a good salesperson, the cart became lighter as sales increased. *Submitted by Sandra Drabik.*

TOLEDO'S OWN TERESA BREWER.

Born Theresa Breuer on May 7, 1931, to a Libbey glass inspector and his home-maker wife, the child star got her start at age two on Toledo's WSPD radio. A performance three years later at the downtown Paramount Theater helped her win a contract to sing on national radio and tour with the acclaimed *Major Bowes Amateur Hour* production until she turned 12. At the time of this head-shot in 1953, Teresa Brewer was soaring into stardom, putting out the year's best-selling record, *"Till I Waltz Again With You."* In a phenomenal career that spanned decades, Toledo's pride and joy recorded nearly 600 songs. *Submitted by Margo (Masney) Fern, fan extraordinaire.*

THE BIG "G" STANDS FOR GIRL POWER.

The General Mills plant in Toledo was one of the area's major employers for over 40 years. Chotty Bruckway (left) was the first female hired by the firm when it opened in the mid-1950s. Rose Parks (on the right) was the third. They are shown here cleaning up in the packaging department where they worked. *Submitted by Chotty (Bruckway) Vergiels.*

FLYING HIGH.

Over 35,000 people attended the opening of Toledo Express Airport on October 31, 1954. Autos parked on the lawn, where the airport would one day feature long-term and short-term parking. The airport now serves as a secondary airport for Detroit, houses the Ohio Air National Guard's 180th Fighter Wing combat-ready F-16C fighter jets and their units, and serves as the main North American hub for BAX Global. Toledo Express was ranked the 31st busiest cargo airport in the United States in 2005. *Submitted by Larry Cousino.*

TOLEDO SOX 1953

"RED" SMITH
General Manager

RAY JOHNSTON
Business Manager

PAUL BRITTIN
Ticket Manager

FRANK GILHOOLEY
Publicity

Left to right—

Back Row: Cerin, Outfielder; Thiel, Pitcher; Reed, Infielder; Hoover, Pitcher; Doc Feran, Trainer; Wall, Pitcher; Estock, Pitcher; Marquez, Outfielder; Queen, Infielder.

Center Row: Montag, Outfielder; Williams, Catcher; Just, Coach; Ertman, Infielder; Selkirk, Manager; Daniels, Outfielder; Bicknell, Pitcher; Klaus, Infielder; Jethroe, Outfielder.

Front Row: Solt, Catcher; Rambone, Infielder; Dubiel, Pitcher; Conley, Pitcher; Kerr, Infielder; Chipman, Pitcher; Jester, Pitcher.

ONCE A HEN, ALWAYS A HEN.

For three years, there were no Mud Hens in Toledo. Under his new regime as manager, "Red" Smith launched a campaign to rechristen the team. The winner, "Glass Sox," was modified to Toledo Sox, but it didn't stick. The name Mud Hens returned and has been the team's moniker ever since. This 1953 photo shows the Hen-less players, managers and staff. *Submitted by Paul Sprouse.*

123

PIECE OF CAKE.

The second shift employees in the packaging department at the Toledo General Mills plant are ready to roll. It is the plant's opening in 1954 and boxes are lined up on the conveyor to receive their first batch of cake mix. In the top row, from left to right are Chotty Vergiels, Rose Parks, Lillian Harris, Ollie Meck and Betty Brewington. In the middle row are Louise Etve, Walt Schumacher and Harry Berbec. In the bottom row are Al Coleman, Dick Vergiels and Ed Kaney. *Submitted by Chotty Vergiels.*

WHAT A DIFFERENCE A YEAR MAKES.

In 1955, the excavation began for the underpass beneath the New York Central Railroad on Dorr Street just east of Upton Avenue. More than 56,000 cubic yards of earth were excavated for the project (top photo). The dirt was delivered to The University of Toledo as fill for a parking lot. Within a year, the Dorr Street overpass was complete (bottom photo), and the chaos of construction was past. Wilbur Newburg took the before and after photos of the site in the 1950s. *Submitted by David Newburg, nephew of Wilbur Newburg.*

READY TO SHIP OUT.

In May 1953, The *South American* awaited its passengers at the Middlegrounds docks located in downtown Toledo where Monroe meets the Maumee River. 250 area high school seniors from six Toledo public high schools boarded the ship for their senior class trip to Port Colbourne, Ontario and Niagara Falls.

Libbey High School senior Bill Russell was among the students who paid $36 for the trip, which included two nights onboard. Card games, contests, dancing and other activities kept the students entertained under the watchful eyes of 14 chaperones.

Bottom left, Scott High School seniors crowded at the rail of the ship in anticipation of a fun trip. Those who have been identified are (back row, from left) William Moore, Wesley Hall, Melvin Thompson, Morris Sample and Edgar Parks (last two unknown). At the front, fourth from left is Virginia Spencer and sixth from left is Marva Topsil. *Submitted by Bill Russell.*

GUARDIAN ANGEL.

Ever wonder who thought up the idea of pinning notes on the shirts of elementary-age students so they wouldn't lose them? This could be the man. Family legend says Toledo beat cop, Marty Stein, initiated the concept after a child accidentally dropped his note and chased it under a bus. On school days, Officer Stein stood guard at the corner of Central and Detroit Avenues, guiding children safely across the intersection to and from Glenwood School. The building behind and to his left in this 1954 photo is a branch of Toledo Trust. *Submitted by Marty's son, Jim Stein*

125

HINKLEMAN'S HOME FOR ARTISTS.

The Toledo Artists Club formed October 24, 1944, to promote arts and crafts created by local talent. For 25 years member artists like Addie LaFrance, shown here with her watercolors on display, met to share creative sparks and hold annual outdoor shows at their "clubhouse" at 3128 Collingwood Blvd. (now part of the campus of the Old West End Academy). But the artists' community got a new home in 1980, thanks to George P. Crosby, who donated 20 acres on Elmer Drive for a public park in 1964, and a little-known director of city welfare and recreation, Elmer Hinkleman. It was Hinkleman's idea to create a center to promote gardening, horticultural education and the arts. Today, Toledo Botanical Garden (originally Crosby Gardens) is home to the Toledo Artists Club and 18 other artisan, horticulture and conservation groups, a sculpture park, and the annual Crosby Festival of the Arts. *Submitted by Addie's daughter, Christine Vischer.*

MOBIL PAINTER.

Before there were computers and automated printing, there was painter Richard Buchele. He held the contract to paint all the Mobil Gas billboards in Ohio and Southern Michigan. Here, in 1955, he is working on the billboard for the Mobil station on Sylvania Avenue and Overland Parkway. Richard devised a paint-by-number system that made it possible for an unskilled painter to assist him without sacrificing the quality of the work. *Submitted by Richard's daughter, Joan Daggett and husband Gerald.*

KEY PUNCHER.

Joanne Colby, third from the left, was a key punch operator at Save Electric in 1954. She is seen posing with fellow employees next to some of the era's "state-of-the-art" business machines. The apparatus on the right under the wall-mounted bins was used to collate papers. The behemoth on the left is an early IBM printer. Save Electric was located at 514 Front Street, the same building that housed the local corn borer office in the 1920s where Joanne's parents worked and met. *Submitted by Joanne Colby.*

PRESSING BUSINESS.

The first-shift employees in the Press Shop of Willys Motors take time away from their duties to pose for a department photo. Standing third from the left in the middle row is Dale Errington. Though an apprentice at the time, Dale would go on to work at the company 33 years. His brother Robert, who shot the photo, also worked in the Press Shop, retiring after 38 years of service. Side and floor panels dangle above the workers, waiting for assembly on a 1955 Willy's vehicle. *Submitted by Dale Errington.*

DON'T CRACK UP!

Jim Rudes and Barbara Krall are broadcasting a live commercial for Hekman's Club Crackers on WSPD TV, Channel 13, in 1955. Broadcasting live had its dangers, but judging from their faces, everything here seems to be going well. Mr. Rudes was a well-known personality on WSPD for several decades, and he later performed in many Toledo theater productions. *Submitted by Pat Rudes, wife of Jim Rudes.*

RADIO ROUNDUP.

Listeners were faithful to WTOL's Country Song Roundup each Saturday evening between 7:30 and 8:00 pm in the early 1950s. That's when Montana Mel and the Sunset Pioneers performed country and western, hillbilly and folk music over the airwaves of Toledo. Pictured, from left, are Bill Stribrny, Mel Jacobs, Bill Mayfield and Bill Cotterman. *Submitted by Jim Stribrny.*

ON THE RIGHT TRACK.

Bobb Vergiels poses next to his one-year-old brother, Bruce, as Mom, Virginia, lends a hand of support in this Christmastime photo from 1955. As an adult, Bobb served as the voice behind a number of organized sports teams, including the Toledo Storm hockey, Detroit Tigers baseball, Detroit Lions football and Michigan Wolverines basketball clubs. *Submitted by Bobb Vergiels.*

WHAT'S IN A NAME?

Terry Staniscewski (left) mugs for the camera circa 1955 after winning the Name the Baby Elephant contest. His suggestion of "Amber" was chosen from the many entries received as the moniker for the recent addition to The Toledo Zoo, a newly born Asian elephant, donated by The Blade. Joining Terry in Toledo Blade's Green Banner Safety Elephant trailer, a tie-in to the contest promoting safe driving, are James and Debra Cann. *Submitted by Robin and Alan Woody.*

BOY, WHAT SCOUTS!

The members of Cub Scout Pack 9 of St. Ann's Church pose for a group portrait outside their den mother's home at 1309 Thatcher Drive in 1956. From left to right, they are Jerry O'Reilly, John Metzger, Gladys O'Reilly, Tom Cousino, Tom Kaiser and Jim O'Reilly. A half century later, that tall Cub on Gladys's right will own and manage some of Toledo's most popular restaurants. *Submitted by Jim O'Reilly.*

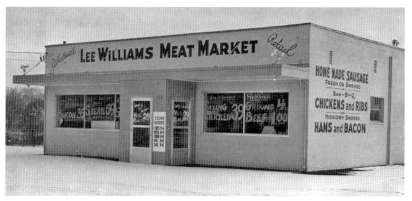

GRADE A TOP-CHOICE.

Barry Willams was a man on a mission: Sell the freshest, highest-quality meats at the best price possible. So, in 1955, he transformed that dream into reality, opening Lee Willams Meat Market at 3002 131st Street. Working long hours but holding true to his ideals, Barry nurtured his modest butcher shop. Today, Lee Willams Meat Market is House of Meats, with a dozen locations in Toledo and Columbus. *Submitted by Mike Crowder, son of Barry Williams.*

LIGHTENING FAST.

Christened the Nicki Too, Bob Trost's sailing beauty was a small swift vessel of the Lightening Class. It was a racing model popular in regattas sponsored by the Toledo Yacht Club in the 1950s. Shown here in this 1956 photo, Bob takes his creation out for a spin with the winds, Point Place and the Club at his back. *Submitted by Bob's wife, Carlene Trost.*

MARCHING UP MADISON.

Former Devilbiss High School band member Carol (Ortman) Newburg captured her team-mates in film as they strutted their stuff up Madison Avenue during an Armed Forces Day parade in 1956 or '57. The Spitzer Building is the second building on the left, next to the band. *Submitted by Carol Newburg.*

LOAD, SET AND FORGET.

Lester Nicolson; his wife, Mae; and daughter, Linda, listen intently as the salesman pitches the new automatic, all-electric clothes dryer. The "How Many Clothespins" contest, featured in this circa 1957 photo, was a marketing ploy to get customers to modernize their way of thinking about drying their clothes. This booth was just one of the many displays at that year's Home Show, held at the Civic Auditorium downtown. From 1927 to the late 60s when it closed, the Auditorium showcased a little of everything, including bridal shows, boxing matches and concerts by the day's top performers. The location is now the home of the Erie Street Market. *Submitted by Mike Crowder.*

STATIONED STATESIDE.

Charles (Chuck) Hickman served as a U.S. Army paratrooper during World War II. Like many "doughboys," he was impressed with the rugged reliability of the Jeeps he'd driven during the war. Once he was back stateside, he came to Toledo to buy a Jeep for himself. By 1947, he owned a Jeep tow truck and a Sohio service station on Detroit Avenue. The station in this photo is his second Sohio business, at Canton Avenue and Jackson Street, probably one of the most lucrative intersections in downtown Toledo. He bought another station in 1956, the year this photo was taken. *Submitted by Chuck's son and daughter-in-law, Bruce & Bev Hickman.*

LOVELY LILLIAN AT LASALLE'S.

Lillian Gregg is pictured here, right, with an unknown lady in the cosmetic department of LaSalle & Koch Department Store about 1957. She worked at LaSalle's for twenty years. The LaSalle's building was a downtown landmark at Adams and Huron since World War I, and is now the LaSalle Apartments. The company was later bought out by Macy's and then Elder-Beerman. *Submitted by Joanne Dearth, daughter of Lillian Gregg.*

MEXICO COMES TO SCHOOL.

Equilla Roach, a 1st grade teacher at Roosevelt Elementary School in Toledo, went to Mexico in 1958 to visit her brother, Navarro Gibson, a student at the University of Mexico in Mexico City. She returned with plenty of souvenirs to help her students learn about Mexico and its culture. Equilla retired after teaching for 35 years. *Submitted by Equilla Roach.*

131

EVEN SANTA SHOPPED AT TIEDTKE'S.

Like many families in Toledo, the Madrykowskis brought little Gene to visit Santa Claus at Tiedtke's in 1957. Tiedtke's on Summit and Adams streets was the nation's first superstore. They had everything – from a bakery to beds, specialty foods to furniture, toys to teapots. Why would Santa go anywhere else? True, Westgate Shopping Center had opened by then, but Tiedtke's was a Toledo tradition. *Submitted by Gene Madrykowski.*

IN HONOR OF A PRINCIPAL.

Patti Jo Bennett and some of the fifth grade class of 1958 pose with their teacher, Mrs. Mary Robert, in front of Marshall Elementary. Originally known as the Newton School because of its location on the corner of Broadway and Newton, it was renamed in 1938 in honor of a much-loved principal, Jessica Marshall, who passed away that year. The first building (shown here) was torn down in 1963, and a new school was built nearby at 415 Colburn. *Submitted by Barbara Douthett, 1958 graduate of Marshall Elementary.*

A WONDER INDEED.

At the midpoint of the 20th Century, The Toledo Zoo boasted one of the most popular children's attractions in the region: Wonder Valley. Located at the bottom of a hill next to the Amphitheater and below the Aquarium, it was home to the usual pet-able animals, plus a few surprises. Children and their parents could enjoy the company of such unexpected pleasures as a giant Galapagos turtle and a St. Bernard Swiss mountain-rescue dog. In this August 10, 1957 photo, young Terry Lee Shier is surrounded by Wonder Valley's ever-hungry herd of goats. *Submitted by Catherine Shier.*

FUELING THE HOLIDAY SPIRIT.

Sunoco got its start in Ohio on March 27, 1886, when Joseph Newton Pew and Edward O. Emerson, partners in The Peoples Natural Gas Company in Pittsburgh, Pa., paid $4,500 for two oil leases near Lima, Ohio. Within a few years the company had acquired pipelines, leases and storage tanks. On March 17, 1890, it became The Sun Oil Company of Ohio. Through the purchase of the Diamond Oil Company in 1894, Sun acquired a refinery in Toledo, Ohio, and began operations there in 1895. By the late 1950s, that refinery had become an East Toledo landmark. In this circa 1959 photo, strings of holiday lights adorn its towers, emitting a festive glow. *Submitted by Alice Verb.*

FROM MAYOR TO GOVERNOR.

TV newsman Jim Rudes, right, interviews Toledo Mayor and later Ohio Governor Mike DiSalle in this 1958 photograph in the WSPD studio. Jim Rudes was a long-time popular Toledo newscaster, and Mike DiSalle, a Central Catholic graduate, was a successful politician, for whom our I-75 bridge is named. *Submitted by Pat Rudes, wife of Jim Rudes.*

10-4, GOOD BUDDY.

It may be 1958, but don't let Henrietta Mierwiak hear you say that a woman's place is in the home. Clearly "Hank" Henrietta had other ideas. With the support of her father, the young woman opened Hank's Truck Stop at King Road and Central Avenue in West Toledo. Offering good food and good service at a good price, the business was a popular stop for over-the-road haulers. Pictured between the two unidentified men (presumed to be uncles) are Henrietta "Hank" Mierwiak and Henrietta Oberthin. *Submitted by Henrietta Mierwiak-Tenney.*

THE RITE STUFF.

These Junior Achievers display a poster for their product, Flavor-Rite salad dressing, at an Open House held at JA headquarters, 136 North Erie St., circa 1950. Lex Youngman, age 18 at the time, was a senior at Woodward High School, and president of Flavor-Rite, a Junior Achievement company sponsored by Ohio Fuel (now Columbia Gas). The young woman next to him was 17-year-old Woodward senior, Rhodena Fulwider. *Submitted by Chris Kozak, Columbia Gas of Ohio.*

FERRY UP THE RIVER.

There was a time in the mid-20th Century when Toledoans could hop a ferry to Boblo Island in Michigan for an evening of entertainment. In addition to the relaxing scenic boat ride, there was the fun of watching traffic come to a halt on the "Cherry Street Bridge" (now known as the Martin Luther King Bridge), as the drawbridge was raised to allow the ferry to pass beneath it. *Submitted by Chotty Vergiels.*

IT'S BEGINNING TO LOOK A LOT LIKE...

The shoppers outside the LaSalle & Koch department store at Adams and Huron look dressed for spring. But the lights are on in the store's arches and the roof of the awning seems adorned with artificial snow and holiday figures. Could the winter gift-giving season be far behind? *Submitted by Chotty Vergiels.*

A BOOK SIGNING AND BANQUET.

Boxing aficionados will recall that Jack Dempsey and Jess Willard fought each other for the heavyweight title in Toledo's Bay View Park in July 1919. Folks gathered early in front of Hirsch's Bookstore, 614 Adams St., on Wednesday, May 17, 1961 in anticipation of meeting Mr. Dempsey and purchasing his newly penned autobiography. The boxer who broke Jess Willard's jaw with one punch on his way to winning the heavyweight championship title in 1919, was returning to the city where it all happened. The autobiography on sale, *Dempsey*, is still considered the authoritative story of Jack Dempsey's life and the boxing industry that he dominated until 1927.

Top Left: Many of the principals gathered in town once again, this time at a banquet in Dempsey's honor at the Commodore Perry Hotel. Brothers Morris and William Hirsch pose with former Heavyweight Champion Jack Dempsey backstage at the banquet. Morris was then-owner of the Hirsch Bookstore. William B. Hirsch was Lucas County Sheriff from 1952-1968. Both were obviously Dempsey fans as they are seen holding copies of the fighter's autobiography.

Top Right: At the banquet, Dempsey is seated at the main table, signing a copy of his autobiography for a fan. Above him at the microphone is Hirsch Bookstore owner Morris Hirsch, with fight promoter Ad Thatcher to his right, followed by Toledo Mayor Michael Damas. *Submitted by Gordon Hirsch; Photographer, Lee Merkle.*

TUPPERWARE DARE.

In the Sixties, Joe Ann Erskine earned a second income for her family as a manager for Tupperware storage containers, sold at in-home parties around Toledo. In 1961, she earned something else, too: a brand new Ford Fairlane 500 to use for two years. Joe Ann was one of the highest distributors of Tupperware in the Toledo area. Tupperware managers all over the country were awarded a car on the same basis as part of a special promotion. Joe Anne and her brood are shown here on Douglas Road in the Wernerts Corners area, accepting keys to her new Ford. Pictured (left to right), are Cynthia Erskine (Rockwell), Scott Erskine, Michael Erskine, Jane Erskine (Cote), Diane Erskine (Johnson), award-winner Joe Ann Erskine, her husband Jim Erskine, local Tupperware distributors Kay and Walt Pease, and two unidentified Tupperware dealers. *Submitted by Joe Ann's daughter, Cynthia (Erskine) Rockwell.*

THIS SCHOOL SAW IT ALL.

You don't have to look any further than their faces to see that teacher Roger L. Stull (background) has his hands full with this class. These are Point Place Junior High students during the 1960 school year. Scott Shook (second row, far right) took this photo. The original school built at 131st and Summit streets had two classrooms. A brick school was built in 1919 for grades one through eight. Then, when new elementary schools were completed in 1930, it became Point Place High School. By the 1940s Point Place had been annexed by Toledo and had too few students for its high school. So the students were switched to Waite High School and the building became Point Place Junior High. The school closed in 1979. *Submitted by Scott and Judy Shook.*

MOM CLASS 101.

A group of new moms gather outside the viewing window of Mercy Hospital's nursery to catch a glimpse of their tiny offspring. The obstetrics department was housed in the hospital's St. Joseph wing, which was added to the hospital's fourth floor in 1940. The facility featured all of the state-of-the-art equipment available in that era – and it operated under the prevailing outlook of the time: Physicians and nurses rather than mothers took responsibility for the care of newborns in the first few days of life. *Submitted by Mercy College of Northwest Ohio.*

MOTHER AND SON BUSINESS.

The recipe for success was simple at the old Suder Inn: serve nothing but quality homemade soup and sandwiches. Owned by the mother-and-son team of Sophie Oberski and Leonard Hoppe, it sat at the corner of Suder and Mayo Streets from 1936 to 1962, when it was razed as part of an urban renewal effort. The family lived upstairs until 1952. *Submitted by Leonard's son, Leonard S. Hoppe.*

PENNIES FROM HEAVEN.

The Hub Bar located at Jackson and St. Clair Streets had a cigarette machine that wouldn't give change. But the bar's owners, brothers Andrew and Chris Grevis, found a way to make it pay. In 1962, cigarettes cost 17¢. Purchasers would deposit two dimes and receive their favorite brand with three pennies taped to the pack. Those pennies could then be donated toward the purchase of

a trampoline for the Boys and Girls Club of Toledo. As the coins accumulated they were traded in for dollar bills that were thumb-tacked to the ceiling until the required amount had been raised. The bar's owners are shown here receiving a certificate of appreciation for their heaven-sent donation. Seated is Homer Hannon from the Boys and Girls Club. Standing, from left to right, are Andrew Grevis, Chris Grevis and Toledo City Councilman Charles Ikes. *Submitted by Chris Grevis and Fay Grevis, wife of Andrew Grevis.*

BABY TIMES TEN.

If you are a photojournalist, what image captures the sentiments of Father's Day more accurately than a dad surrounded by his loving children – all nine of them? Actually, Frank, the smiling man in the center of the action, would eventually sire ten children. But on Father's Day 1962, his youngest, Thomas, has yet to make an appearance. The rest of the brood is pictured clockwise starting at the top: Kurt (striped shirt), Joan, Debra, Jane, baby Michael, Mark, Barbara and Kristine. Paul is peeking over dad's head. This photo was taken by Blade photographer Jack Ackerman.
Submitted by Mike Gessner.

139

REALLY, REALLY BIG.

Tiedtke's Department Store was famous for its big, innovative promotions. This is one of their biggest – the annual Giant Birthday Sale. In this 1962 photo, three-year-old Suzanne Klein holds the hand of 7'4" Jakob Nacken, a very tall gentleman in front of the Tiedtke's lunch counter. Just ten years later, Tiedtke's closed, leaving Toledo with one giant heartbreak. *Submitted by Suzanne Melchior.*

LAGOS LEGACY.

The year was 1965, five years after their father retired and closed the family store, Lagos Market. The Lagos children, (left to right), Helen, owner of the Bee Gay Inn in East Toledo; George, Jr., salesman for the Star Vending Company; Anna, employee at Libbey-Owens-Ford; and Mary, director of the Patrician Stevens Career College and Finishing School; got together for a libation at Helen's thriving bar in the old Ironwood neighborhood. *Submitted by George's daughter, Sharon Lagos Bullion.*

HAPPY BIRTHDAY TO US.

Louis Heilbrun cuts a piece of the piece de resistance he and fellow Tiedtke Department Store master bakers prepared for customers to enjoy as they celebrated the store's birthday in 1962. The six-story downtown landmark, on the northeast corner of Summit and Adams Streets since 1910, never did anything on a small scale, much to the delight of Toledoans for over 60 years. The 72-sheet giant cake weighed 1,000 pounds, was nine feet tall and took 50 hours to make. In making their masterpiece, the bakers used 100 quarts of milk, 200 pounds of flour, 225 pounds of sugar, 1200 eggs and 125 pounds of shortening. And to top it off: 200 pounds of heavenly frosting. *Submitted by Louis Heilbrun and his wife, Vera.*

PAPER MISTER?

Larry Parker was just eight years old when this photo was taken on November 10, 1960, but he was already an old hand at delivering The Blade. He poses here next to a Times newspaper rack on the corner of Superior and Jackson. He had started selling papers at the age of five, working with his cousin six days a week to make sure everybody got the news. *Submitted by Larry Parker, Sr.*

141

SUPER SHOPPER.

As the Grand Prize winner in the Pepsi-Cola Shoppers Sweepstakes, Donna Mack was given fifteen minutes to shop till she dropped in her favorite A&P Supermarket. So on July 11, 1963, people from around the area converged on the store at 1200 Sylvania Avenue, near Willys Parkway, to watch. At precisely 8:30 a.m. Donna took off running, filling twenty carts with foodstuffs totaling $796.23. It took twenty minutes to ring up her winnings. *Submitted by Donna Mack.*

TIMBER!

It was fortunate no cars were driving along Collingwood Blvd. during the 1963 June storm that brought this tree crashing into the road. With the weather finally clear, the neighborhood kid patrol has gathered to assess the damage. Behind them to the right stands the old UAW Local 12 CIO union hall near the corner of Winthrop St. *Submitted by Pat O'Brien*

GENTLEMEN, START YOUR ENGINES.
These snazzy new Dodge automobiles are lined up along Madison Avenue in this 1963 photograph advertising Champion Spark Plug's highway safety program. Reddish Dodge, owned by Dick Reddish, was at 1107 Madison. Champion leased cars to Reddish that were driven by Indy Car race drivers. In this photograph are, left to right, Nolan Vogelpohl, Mr. Stranahan, and Bob Dupont. *Submitted by Janet Vogelpohl.*

DON'T WORRY, BE HAPPY.
The Bee Gay Inn, a Hungarian bar in the old Ironwood neighborhood of East Toledo, was quite busy in March, 1964. Located at 1328 Liberty Street at White, the Bee Gay was always well-stocked. Helen Myrice, the owner, is seated second from the left, and the bar, still in business today, later became known as Helen's. *Submitted by Alice Verb, who worked as a housekeeper there from the 1960s until 1993.*

AND ALL THAT JAZZ.
With the opening of her first club in 1963, Rusty's Music Bar at 3330 Secor Road, Margaret "Rusty" Monroe set the stage for turning Toledo into a jazz haven. The transition in 1979 to Rusty's Jazz Café on Tedrow Road established the venue's standing as one of the few premiere nightclubs in the country to cater exclusively to jazz artists and fans. Rusty's went on to earn its reputation as a favorite stomping ground for nationally acclaimed artists and a launching pad for up-and-coming musicians with appearances by Wynton Marsalis, Maynard Ferguson, Lionel Hampton, Cannonball Adderly and others. Despite her retirement in 2003, Jazz lovers the world over continue to sing the praises of "Toledo's First Lady of Jazz" for her contributions to the music genre. *Submitted by Margaret "Rusty" Monroe.*

143

PALM SUNDAY TWISTER.

It was the evening of April 12, 1965, when a twister ripped through the Toledo area, toppling trees, hefting boats out of the water along Ottawa River Road and cutting power to thousands of Toledoans. Quickly dubbed the "Palm Sunday Tornado", the storm confined much of its devastation to the Point Place area, but other neighborhoods did not escape unscathed. This photo captures the damage in front of Dolly Moriarty's home on Eleanor Avenue. *Submitted by Rob Rowe.*

WE'LL MISS YOU, JOSEPH.

If Joseph Barnett hardly seemed dressed for work, it's because he wasn't. Joseph was sporting his Sunday best in honor of his last day at Dana Corporation – Spicer Division on Bennett Road at Sylvania Avenue. After more than 40 years as a set-up man, loading the die machine for stamping, Mr. Barnett said good-bye to the job he loved; hopefully so he could spend more time on another passion: fishing. *Submitted by Kenneth Barnett, son of Joseph Barnett.*

CLEANING UP IN 1967.

The Jung family owned the Hong Yick Hand Laundry on Adams Street, near 12th, during the 1960s. And it truly was a family business in every sense of the word. As each of the Jung's four children reached the teenage years, Lena, Lizina, Gina and Quentin could be found amidst the piles of clothes, tagging drop-offs and fetching pick-ups. *Submitted by Barbara Bonofigilio for Peter Talty.*

EQUAL EDUCATION NOW!

Toledo had its share of unrest during the years of civil rights demonstrations in the 1960s. These marchers for equal education in Toledo Public Schools are headed down Collingwood Boulevard in June of 1967. Norton's Hardware is in the background, across from the State Theater at Machen Street. The march was one of several that summer, which led to the postponement of a late July visit by Dr., Martin Luther King, Jr., to September 22. *Submitted by Peter Talty.*

A KING AT SCOTT HIGH.

The man walking from his folding chair toward the podium (sixth from left, under the Bulldogs sign) is Dr. Martin Luther King, Jr. More than 3,500 Toledoans came to hear him speak at the Scott High School fieldhouse on September 22, 1967, sponsored by the local Southern Christian Leadership Conference chapter. Dr. King was shot and killed the following April in Memphis, four years after receiving the Nobel Peace Prize for his unwavering practice of nonviolence in the struggle for civil rights. *Submitted by Peter Talty.*

END OF AN ERA.

At 13 acres, the Wright Brothers Greenhouse was the largest one-unit greenhouse in the country. Founded in 1905 by Ed Wright and his brother, Arthur G. Wright, the company prospered under three generations of family leadership, providing thousands of tons of tomatoes and lettuce to cities across the U.S. annually. But as freight rates and the cost of doing business rose, the business eventually floundered. The massive greenhouse was closed in 1965 and was razed in 1966. This 1966 photo shows the demolition site, as viewed from Cheltenham facing Bancroft, UT's University Hall and the Ritter Planetarium. *Submitted by Ed Wright III.*

COME SAIL AWAY...

The Lamson's Department Store on Jefferson and Erie was a popular downtown shopping destination, but never more so than when it displayed the sailboat skippered by Ohioan Robert Manry. Only 13.5 feet long, the Tinkerbelle carried Manry from Falmouth, Massachusetts to Falmouth, England in 78 days in the summer of 1965. At the time, it was the smallest boat to have ever crossed the Atlantic. It was a record-breaking feat of incredible proportions, especially when you saw how frighteningly small the vessel looked amidst the counters and clothing on Lamson's main floor in February 1966. *Submitted by Peter Talty.*

CONTROVERSIAL CANDIDATE.

Former governor of Alabama, George Wallace, spoke in Toledo at the Whitmer High School field house on November 9, 1967 during his campaign for the 1968 presidential election. He spoke behind his own customized lectern with quarter-inch bulletproof armor plate beneath its mahogany veneer. Hecklers, who arrived early for front-row seats, were removed by Toledo policemen. An estimated 3,500 people attended. Wallace was best known for his pro-segregation views during the American desegregation period. While campaigning in Maryland on May 15, 1972, Wallace was shot five times by would-be assassin Arthur Bremer. This left him paralyzed. He died on September 13, 1998 of septic shock from a bacterial infection. He had also suffered from Parkinson's disease, respiratory problems and complications from his gunshot spinal injury. *Submitted by Peter Talty.*

A FAMILY'S MARCH FOR FREEDOM.

Social unrest rocked our nation in 1968. The Democratic National Convention in Chicago and university campuses across the country were engulfed by angry protestors of the Vietnam War. At the same time, hundreds of thousands shared in the spirit of Martin Luther King, Jr. and demonstrated nationwide for the full civil and political rights of African Americans. Closer to home, a Toledo family banded together in a show of similar support, carrying signs and waving banners in the local Freedom March. In this photo taken that day, University Hall's bell tower, rising up from the campus of the University of Toledo, flanks fellow marchers (from left) Blaine Campbell (in white suit), Jaclyn (Palmer) Roach, Mz. Diva (age 12), Kamal Najib (young boy holding sign over right shoulder), Jonetta Campbell (in glasses above Kamal) and Elouise Campbell (to Jonetta's left). *Submitted by Mz. Diva.*

ALL EYES ARE ON...

Students of Patricia Stevens Career College and Finishing School gather at the school on Superior Street above Dyers Restaurant. They have evidently returned from one of many modeling competitions; note the tiara/crown worn by the young lady second from left and the floral arrangements with each girl. Mary L. Mather, owner and director of the school, stands back row, second from right. Known by stu-

dents and the modeling industry as Miss LaRue, Mary ran the school from 1955 to 1978. The school was moved to Erie St. in 1968. The move was speeded up when local burlesque queen Rose LaRose moved her revue to the Esquire Theater, directly across the street from the finishing school. The school closed its doors after 24 years and nearly 10,000 graduates. *Submitted by Mary's daughter, Christine Mather Bothe.*

RACY AND RUGGED.

Deemed the "rugged rascal only Toledo could build", this Jeepster Convertible was proudly dsplayed in 1968 by Patricia Stevens Finishing School models (names unknown). Features included a continental spare, hot new V-6 with automatic transmission and with one flip of the lever – it became a 4-wheel drive. Not that this was needed along Toledo's downtown riverfront, but it was fun to have. *Submitted by Christine Mather Bothe, daughter of Mary Mather, owner and director of Patricia Stevens Career and Finishing School.*

FIGHT NIGHT.
A professional boxing tournament held in Toledo's Civic Auditorium in 1968 brought together an impressive threesome of the sport's heavyweights. From left to right are former heavyweight champion Joe Louis, boxing promoter Sid Goldberg, his grandson Andy Goldberg, son Albert Goldberg, and former world featherweight champion Willie Pep. Louis and Pep were guest referees at the event. *Submitted by Albert Goldberg.*

A HOWLING GOOD TIME.

From left to right, young Anna Losoya and her cousins, Rene and Tina Losoya, grab front row seats at The Toledo Zoo's Polar Bear habitat, circa June 1968. One bear is serenading visitors – an unusual occurrence among the taciturn animals. There was a time, however, when guests would toss graham crackers and marshmallows to the bears in an attempt to make them sit up and beg. Although animal keepers cracked down on the practice, the beasts themselves took a while longer to adjust. This may have been a very vocal complaint over the recent ban on snacks. *Submitted by Kathleen Mack, mother of Anna Losoya.*

PUT 'ER THERE.

Eight-year-old Amy Rudes (Walton) is greeted by a baby elephant at the Toledo Zoo in this August 1967 photo. The petting zoo at that time was known as Wonder Valley, which was down the hill at the right of the Broadway entrance. *Submitted by Pat Rudes, mother of Amy.*

GOING ON ZOOFARI.

For over 100 years, the Toledo Zoo has entertained and enlightened visitors of all ages. Sisters Jeanne and Kathy Kaslly take time out in August of 1968 to ride the elephant, just one of the many carved stone animals that prowl the playground area, before heading over to the polar bear exhibit (background). *Submitted by Naomi Sommers, aunt of Jeanne and Kathy Kaslly.*

PRIMED FOR "POM AND CIRCUMSTANCE."

Graduates of Thomas A. DeVilbiss High School and their guests congregate outside the The University of Toledo Field House in 1968. The high school, which opened in 1931, was part of the Toledo Public School District and served primarily the Old Orchard neighborhood. DeVilbiss and other local high schools often used the Field House, which served as UT's gymnasium and one of the city's premiere venues for athletic events, graduation ceremonies and concerts. Amid the cavalcade of caps and gowns, waiting eagerly to see Ken Harris receive his diploma, are (forefront, from left) Kitty Robinson, Ken's sister Ellen Harris (Lewis) and an unidentified friend. Thomas A. DeVilbiss High School closed in 1991, though the building still remains on Upton Avenue near Central. *Submitted by Richard Bomer, grandson of Kitty Robinson.*

SHE DID IT ALL.

The year was 1968 and not only was Jane Welborn a full-time mother of three children under the age of 10, but she was also a college student at UT. Classes must have seemed a refreshing break after taking care of a household, a husband and family, and working part-time at JC Penney, Miracle Mile. Jane graduated with a bachelors degree in education and went on to teach 30 years – 29 for the Toledo Public School system. She taught both second and third grades at Navarre Elementary, finally retiring in 1998. *Submitted by Sara E. Welborn, her favorite daughter, designer of this book, and the ugly duckling standing to the right of her mother.*

WAIT, DON'T I KNOW YOU?

Toledo Firefighter, Tom Stevenson, Jr., played Santa at Lamson's department store for several years during the 1960s. In December 1969, his father Tom Stevenson, Sr., paid him a visit. Tom Sr.'s daughter (and Santa's sister), Nancy Lee Foster, has no idea what he asked for. *Submitted by Nancy Lee Foster.*

THE GROWTH OF A SYNAGOGUE.

The burgeoning congregation of B'nai Jacob voted to merge with Toledo's second Orthodox Jewish community, Sharizedeck, in 1979. Closing their respective synagogues – B'nai Jacob's at Parkwood and W. Bancroft, and Sharizedeck at Mulberry and Moore – the two communities became Etz Chayim and built a new synagogue on Woodley Rd. Etz Chayim means "tree of life", and some of the fruits of that tree are visible here: the confirmation class of 1970. *Submitted by Sharon Rainwasser*

CHRISTMAS KITSCH.

Bursting onto the mod holiday decorating scene in the early 1960s, the aluminum Christmas tree came in a variety of sizes and colors. This artificial silver tree adorns a table at Jo & Paul Shook's home on 299th Street in Point Place in December 1970. Scott Shook, with his fiancee Judy Lebowsky, is opening presents to celebrate his December graduation from the University of Toledo with a degree in Business Administration. *Submitted by Judy Lebowsky Shook.*

154

SUBMITTER INDEX

WE REALLY DELIVER.
Crisply attired in uniforms and hats, Blade newspaper drivers line up next to their vehicles along Orange Street outside The Toledo Blade building. Little about that edifice has changed over the years, although the buildings behind it are mostly gone. Today, the Toledo Fire Department headquarters fills the open space. *Submitted by Ken Pool.*